# dow...

 *a beginner's guide*

NAOMI OZANIEC

# Hodder & Stoughton

A MEMBER OF THE HODDER HEADLINE GROUP

Orders: please contact Bookpoint Ltd, 39 Milton Park, Abingdon, Oxon OX14 4TD.
Telephone: (44) 01235 400414, Fax: (44) 01235 400454. Lines are open from
9.00–6.00, Monday to Saturday, with a 24-hour message answering service.
Email address: orders@bookpoint.co.uk

*British Library Cataloguing in Publication Data*
A catalogue record for this title is available from The British Library

ISBN 0 340 73750 6

First published 1994
This edition published 1999
Impression number    10  9  8  7  6  5  4  3  2  1
Year                 2004  2003  2002  2001  2000  1999

Typeset by Wearset, Boldon, Tyne and Wear
Printed in Great Britain for Hodder & Stoughton Educational, a division of Hodder
Headline Plc, 338 Euston Road, London NW1 3BH by Cox & Wyman Ltd, Reading,
Berkshire

# CONTENTS

# INTRODUCTION

D owsing is an old and well-established practice which is now enjoying something of a revival. Water divining has never quite faded from country life. There is nothing 'supernatural' about dowsing for water. Professional dowsers are often the most down to earth people imaginable. Children frequently pick up dowsing without any difficulty. Dowsing is a skill which can be learned and applied. As you learn more about dowsing, you also learn about yourself and your surroundings.

The earliest written reports about dowsing come from Germany. According to Georg Bauer, more commonly known as Georgius Agricola, sixteenth century German miners dowsed for metallic ores. In *De Re Metallica* he wrote, 'It is said that the moment they place their feet on a vein the twig immediately turns and twists and so by its action discloses the vein; when they move their feet again and go away from that spot the twig becomes once more immobile.' The Germans called the dowsing twig 'the wishing rod'. No doubt all the miners were wishing that it would make their fortune. In the Harz mountains of northern Germany, miners used this technique for hundreds of years to locate veins of gold, copper, and iron. The miners of Rammelsberg and Erzgebirge also used dowsing in their daily work. Mine dowsers enjoyed an extremely high status in Germany. They were even trained to a certain standard and were awarded a diploma on reaching the requirements.

We can only assume that dowsing proved successful for them. It is impossible to imagine hard-headed mining men pursuing something without a pay-off at the end of the day. These men were only interested in results. As mining became more important, so the fame

of this technique spread too. It reached England where Elizabeth I had encouraged German mining expertise. In 1639 Gabriel Plattes explained how to cut rods and use them for locating metallic ores.

> *They tell us something strange and odd,*
> *About a certain Magick Rod,*
> *That, bending down its Top, divines*
> *When e'er the Soil has Golden Mines:*
> *Where there are none, it stands erect,*
> *Scorning to show the least Respect.*

The miners of the Mendip Hills particularly took to this new practice. They used dowsing in the search for zinc and lead. The practice was common enough to attract the attention of the scientist Robert Boyle. His scientific curiosity was sufficiently aroused for him

Use of a divining rod, from *Agricola's Treatise on Mining*, 1557

to undertake some on-site investigation. He wrote: 'One gentleman who lives near the lead mines in Somersetshire, leading me over those parts of the mines where he knew that metallic veins did run, made me take note of the stooping of the Wand, when he passed over a Vein of Oar and protested that the motion of his hand did not contribute to the indications of the wand, but that sometimes he held it so fast, it would bend so strongly as to break in his hand.' (*New Light on an Ancient Art*, by Tom Williamson.)

Boyle in fact undertook some experiments of his own. However, he did not have much success himself and concluded that the wand did not work for everyone. As a scientist he found himself in a curious position. He had seen the success in the hands of others but could not reproduce the same success in his own hands. 'When my opinion is ask'd of those things, I dare not peremptorily reject and yet am not convinced of, namely that they have seen them can much more reasonably believe them than they have not.'

Dowsing also attracted interest in Cornwall, a county with a long mining history. William Pryce of Redruth became a great authority on Cornish mining. He wrote *Mineralogia Cornubiensis* which included a detailed report about the use of dowsing. The report was written by his friend the pioneering industrialist William Cookworthy. Cookworthy reported that local miners made their dowsing rods from a single forked hazel twig or other wood. This rod was unusually long by modern standards, between two and a half and three feet. He commented that they sometimes tied separate shoots together. Cookworthy himself seemed to have a good understanding of the dowsing process. He wrote that the best results were achieved in a certain state of mind. 'A man ought to hold the rod with the same indifference and inattention to, or reasoning about it or its effect, as he holds a fishing rod or a walking stick.' He noted that the rod 'constantly answers in the hands of peasants, women and children who hold it simply without puzzling their minds with doubts or reasoning.' Cookworthy was a practical and successful industrialist. His interest was not metaphysical but primarily commercial. He was convinced that it was possible to dowse successfully for lode bearing veins. Pryce, too, recorded many local success stories.

The popularity of dowsing declined somewhat in the eighteenth century. No-one was able to produce a satisfying theory to explain how it worked. This left it open to charges of diabolic influence. By the time the diabolic theory had been itself discredited, mining technology too had moved on. However, in a curious reversal of fortunes, dowsing enjoyed a brief resurgence among the geologists of the USSR as it was called in the 1960s. A small group of interested dowser-geologists began to experiment for themselves. They even developed a new style dowsing implement. This rod revolves in the hands. The team even designed an automatic revolution counter to record the number of turns made by the rod over a given distance. The high-tech dowsing device had arrived at last! Despite the surge of enthusiasm and some undoubted successes, the western mining industry remains unmoved and unwilling to supply either time or research capital. Once again the practice of dowsing is held back because there is no accepted scientific theory. However, the times are changing fast. Science itself is changing fast.

# ḥow ḋoes it work?

Anyone who takes the trouble can prove to their own satisfaction that dowsing does work. However, the baffling question remains the same as ever. How does it work? Every age has produced its own theories in the light of the prevailing scientific understanding. The early identification between dowsing and mining meant that all early explanations were focused on this relationship. It was originally believed that the mineral veins emitted some kind of corpuscles that caused the dowser's rod to dip.

The Jesuit Athanius Kircher attempted to isolate such corpuscles. He balanced dowsing rods of various woods close to a range of metals: of course nothing happened. Kirchner concluded that the dowser was duped by the power of his own imagination. Ironically this conclusion is far nearer to our contemporary understanding of dowsing which stresses the value of the imagination as a positive factor. Pierre Le Lorrain Abbé de Vallemont wrote a treatise in 1693. He recognised that dowsing ability varied from person to person. He

was able to conclude that the dowser played a part in the process. He suggested that the rod served to magnify the body's natural response. His treaty was placed on the prohibited list in 1702 by the Holy See. Other clergymen set out to discredit dowsing, ironically enough by taking two quite contrary positions. On the one hand they tried to show that dowsing did not work; on the other, when it did work, it was made successful by the Devil himself.

Barthélemy Bléton, a famous French dowser, was employed by Marie Antoinette to site wells at Versailles. His work attracted controversy, typical of the mixed attitude of the time. The astronomer Joseph-Jerome de Laland was brought in as a representative of the scientific community to put Bléton to the test. Laland denounced the dowser as a fraud on the grounds that Bléton caused the rod to move with his own fingers. The scientific community was determined to separate the operator from the operation. This view is the logical outcome of a purely reductionist viewpoint.

I remember being subjected to exactly the same logic. I became interested in dowsing when I was 11. I experimented with great enthusiasm. My fervour was suitably damped when I too was 'put to the test'. According to the rational and logical view upheld in our household, dowsing could only be proven if it could be seen that the pendulum could move without my helping hand. A suitably scientific test was devised for me. The pendulum was duly suspended over a wooden rod and I was allowed to touch the cord only where it touched the support. It was no surprise to me that the pendulum did not move under these new 'scientific' conditions. However, according to the prevalent 'scientific' view my dowsing had been disproven. I am only grateful that my life did not depend on such a test. My failure did not, however, stop me from dowsing but it did make me question the scientific framework which had failed to provide a proper explanation.

Laland failed to understand that the operator is the key to the process. The same misunderstanding is still encountered today with the cry, 'But, I saw you moving your hand!' The proper answer to this is 'Of course you saw my hand move, how else do you think dowsing works!' It cannot be said often enough, the pendulum has no power of its own. The pendulum does not move on its own. The operator enables the pendulum to move. The success or failure of dowsing should be judged by the result of the particular operation. The degree of movement in the operator's hand is quite irrelevant and should never be used as the criterion for failure or success. If I set out to locate an object and fail, then that particular dowsing experience may be deemed to have failed. If I locate the object then that operation may be deemed successful. In either case the hand movement of the operation as perceived by others is of no consequence. When you start to dowse practically, you can guarantee that someone nearest and dearest to you will attempt to pour cold water on your enthusiasm with those very words, 'But I saw your hand move'. So be prepared.

When we look at the results achieved by dowsers, not at their hand movements, we can begin to examine the claims of dowsing properly. While the French continued to follow the lead set by Laland, the English took a more pragmatic approach. The Director-General of the British Geological Survey, Sir Archibald Geikie, made a careful study of dowsing and concluded that the evidence in favour of dowsing was striking.

Dowsing theories have ranged all the way from the pseudo-scientific to the ridiculous. Historically the church did its best to align dowsing with the Devil and all things evil. In truth dowsing is such an astounding ability that it is not easy to explain. It is so simple that a child can dowse, so accurate that it can be truly bewildering. Scientists and psychologists alike have offered their speciality as a means of explaining dowsing. Scientists have generally been willing to hand the knotty problem over to those specialising in the mind. Traditional science has so far failed to incorporate dowsing. What might be expected from the traditional mind-sciences?

An early investigator was DH Rawcliffe. He was happy to explain dowsing successes with reference to sensory environmental clues such as soil colour, variety of plants, even texture and dampness of the soil. In other words the operator relates to a combination of localised clues. This seems a very poor and inadequate explanation. Some have argued that walking over a geological fault causes a muscle contraction to take place. Dr Solco Tromp believed that

mineral veins and faults produce a muscle reflex, though he was not able to explain the mechanism by which this takes place. Two researchers, Dr Evon Vogt and Dr Ray Hyman at last managed to pinpoint the key issue. 'The unconscious muscular reaction results from a suggestion from the subconscious of the diviner.' Here at last the two significant factors are brought together, the subconscious mind and the muscular reaction. This relationship is the key to all dowsing.

# The subconscious mind

Once we have acknowledged the importance of the subconscious, dowsing becomes so much more than a means of locating either water or minerals, valuable as these abilities may be. If the dowsed reflex accurately mirrors the unconscious mind, then we have access, albeit through a limited means of communication, to the unconscious mind. This can only be a healthy development. It was Jung himself who bemoaned the devaluing of the unconscious mind. He recognised that the unconscious has no voice of its own but speaks through symbol, imagination and dream. It is also perfectly clear from more recent work that the unconscious speaks continuously through the body. Feelings and emotions are expressed through body language, symptoms and even through illness. This continuous interaction shows us that beneath the rational intellect, another dialogue is constantly functioning. Dowsing may put us in touch with this dialogue.

There has been a regrettable tendency to treat the subconscious as a kind of personal dustbin where all unwanted and painful memories are stored. On the contrary the subconscious is a great ally. When the unconscious and conscious mind are in conflict, it becomes difficult if not impossible to achieve the goal. Giving up smoking or losing weight are commendable aspirations. However if intentions are only lodged at the conscious intellectual level, conflict will bring failure. The conscious mind will agree to accept particular targets, but the unconscious mind will subtly undermine personal effort. Failure will be accompanied by self justification and a loss of confidence. Perhaps we might learn to use dowsing as a check on our own deep motives. We need to have the support of the deep mind in the achievement of any long term goals and plans.

Early investigators were quite unable to understand the power that the mind actually plays in the dowsing process. They were locked into the belief system of their own time. We may look at dowsing with the benefit of contemporary insights into the nature of matter and the working of the mind, but it is undoubtedly true that we have not yet learned everything there is to know about the dowsing phenomenon. We need to recognise that we too are locked into the belief system of our time. However, we are blessed to live at the threshold of a new synthesised appreciation between the scientific and the spiritual, the physical and the psychological, the material and the immaterial. Perhaps dowsing can help us expand our own personal understanding of such things.

If we are to understand and apply dowsing in our lives, we have to expand our vision of the world in which we live. We are all deeply and unconsciously influenced by the predominant view of reality. There is no doubt that definitions shift to reflect new balances between religious and scientific thinking. We live in an interesting and important time in the evolutionary understanding of matter. New fields of research show very clearly that matter is neither solid nor permanent, but in a constant state of motion and change. The alien world of subatomic particles shows us that our seemingly solid material world arises from a sea of energies in constant collision. Matter and energy cannot be separated. Matter and energy still hold many mysteries. We live amidst an extraordinary, dynamic continuous wonder. We see only a fraction of this truly magical interchange through our five senses and we are deceived into believing that our partial view is a whole view.

Dowsing enables us to explore the strange world of matter, energy and consciousness. We may set up experiments in the spirit of scientific investigation, we may explore the in-between world of changing energies, we may simply have fun. We will, however, never be bored. We may even make some significant personal discoveries, and we will certainly learn something about ourselves and the world in which we live.

It is very clear that mental powers play a vital part in dowsing. This was made especially clear to me quite recently. While on holiday in the States I spent some time showing my sister-in-law how to dowse. She was convinced that she could not dowse and would never be able to learn. I wondered whether my ability to dowse could in some way be transferred, so we sat very close together. We each had a pendulum. I set my pendulum moving in a strong clockwise rotation. I placed my spare hand on the hand in which she held her pendulum. For a while her pendulum did little, but gradually it picked up a clockwise rotation so that the two seemed to move as if they were magnetically aligned. We experimented like this for a while. When both pendulums had settled into a synchronised rhythm, I began to really concentrate on the movement of my own pendulum. There is no doubt that I was focusing my mind on my pendulum. In my mind I visualised a single orbit, which sustained both pendulums. After a few minutes of sustained and very intense thought, I experienced a sudden surge of energy. It happened instantly. In the same moment, the gyration which my pendulum had been tracing suddenly went into a new orbit. The strong but dignified circle suddenly shifted gear, the pendulum now rose up, spinning like a centrifuge. I could feel the intensity of its movement. Without warning, the pendulum spun out of my hand and landed on the far side of the room. We were both amazed and in truth I felt a little drained.

The mind is complex. It is perfectly clear that we, as human beings, function at many levels. We think and we dream, we create and we imagine, we concentrate and we daydream. We have a conscious mind and an unconscious mind. We have a rational deductive brain. We have an irrational creative brain. We use only a small portion of our brain power. Dowsing is in many ways a curious phenomenon. There is little doubt that it is an unconscious response. Dowsing works best for people who are open to their unconscious levels. Such people dream vividly, follow hunches and are open to feelings. It has to be said that ideally we should be in touch with both intellect and intuition, thinking rationality and irrationality. Unfortunately we live in a society which places an undue emphasis on the intellect and deductive thinking at the expense of the imagination and symbolic thought. People who find it

hard to dowse are invariably those locked into the functions of the left-hand brain. Prizing the intellect, they devalue the intuition and take their own difficulties with dowsing as proof of its dubious nature. Cookworthy's observation that the rod 'constantly answers in the hands of peasants, women and children who hold it simply without puzzling their minds with doubts or reasonings,' is highly significant. It is in fact the first key to mastering dowsing. If we are to dowse with success, we need simplicity and directness. We need to become as children. We have to give up the suspicions and convoluted rationalisations of the adult mind.

# Life-fields

Everything that lives emanates its own life-field. Science is now beginning to show us these emanations. It was Harold S Burr, Professor of Yale, who first spoke of 'the L-Field', and it still seems to be an appropriate term. Burr wrote, 'Electro-dynamic fields are invisible and intangible and it is hard to visualise them.' He attempted to explain how the L-Fields function with a simple analogy. 'When a cook looks at a jelly mould she knows the shape of the jelly she will turn out.' In other words, form follows the energy pattern.

Burr claimed that the L-Field could be detected and examined by measuring the different voltage between two points on, or close to, the surface of the living form. He measured the L-Field in people by placing one electrode on the forehead and the other on the chest. Alternatively he dipped the index finger of each hand in saline solution connected to a vacuum tube voltmeter. He applied this principle to a wide variety of subjects. He discovered that malignancy in the ovary followed an abnormal electrical reading. He experimented with seedlings and was able to predict which ones would develop into healthy plants and which ones would not. He even conducted an experiment using a number of trees in a forest. He drilled two holes in trees, one above the other, a little apart, and inserted wires. He found that the same electrical pattern was followed across the forest. Furthermore, changes in voltage took

place in regular cycles which correlated to the moon. In another experiment, Burr found that faster growing trees such as maple have a somewhat higher electrical potential than the slower growing elm and oak.

Burr was not the first to attempt to understand these invisible fields. He called it an L-Field, others have called it 'bioplasma'. Kirlian's high voltage electrical photography has now shown us images: coronas around fingers, flares around plants, and luminescence around seeds. A Kirlian camera uses no lenses: the photographic image is recorded on film by placing an object in a high tension. In a high frequency electric field the object lies on a sheet of film placed on an insulated plate electrode. In 1939 Semyon Kirlian discovered that he could leave an image of his hand on film shortly after receiving a mild electrical shock. The Kirlian image is clearly an artefact of the electrical field. Nevertheless, like disclosing fluid, the image shows us something that is already present. These discoveries are only a beginning. A relationship between the state of health and energy discharge is already clear. Many important questions remain unanswered. We need to understand the relationship between the form and its Life-Field more fully. Do changes in the L-Field precede or follow physical changes? What more may be learned about the relationship between health and disease? Such questions are pertinent to our study of dowsing. Dowsing is one observed response which takes place as two or more Life-Fields interact. The Life-Field of the operator interacts with the L-Field of the subject being dowsed. We need to understand as much as possible about these L-Fields.

It is not difficult to imagine how a living plant, an animal or a great tree might produce its own life-field. It is more difficult to conceive that an inorganic object such as a stone or a metal might also produce a field of force. Yet if we begin to think more deeply and ask ourselves, 'What is stone, what is metal?' we might come closer and will soon realise that even the most solid and inert of materials are formed of molecules, atoms and in constant and extraordinary motion. Rudimentary physics informs us that the differences we perceive between various materials are in fact deep differences of molecular structure. Each element of the Elementary Table has its

own unique characteristics. When we remind ourselves that all matter is the exteriorisation of extraordinary molecular and atomic processes, then we can begin to appreciate that even inert material may produce another unique characteristic: its own energy signature.

Tom Lethbridge was a pioneer in the field of dowsing. By training he was an archaeologist. He managed to combine his two interests in unique ways. He too was interested in the idea of energy fields. His inventive mind led him to conduct many off-beat experiments. He was interested in the shape and size of the energy field relative to its object. He dowsed for objects at specified distances in order to ascertain the limits of the field. He placed a brass ash tray on the floor of his hall and dowsed for it from upstairs. He placed the ash tray upstairs and dowsed downstairs for it. In both instances he was able to detect an energy field belonging to brass. However, in both cases the energy field was considerably reduced in size. This led him to the extraordinary conclusion that energy fields are conical, extending both above and below the object that we are able to see. His continuing experimentation produced an even more startling conclusion. He placed an object on the floor and plotted the diameter of its force field as dowsed on the floor above. He discovered that the apex of the cone was not static but moved. He concluded that, 'cones appear to swing ahead of the movement of the moon'. Such simple experiments can surely be duplicated if anyone is interested enough to put such hypotheses to the test. We should not scoff at such experiments or dismiss them out of hand. Science is based on observation. Perhaps it is time to conduct some off-beat experiments of our own.

# TOOLS AND TECHNIQUES

*Dowsing is a way of using the body's own reflexes to help you interpret the world around you.*

Tom Graves, The Dowser's Workbook

Dowsing requires no expensive equipment. In fact you can learn to dowse for free, using nothing more than a twig cut from a hedge, a weight on a thread or a simple pendulum. The most important tool is you. The responses given by any dowsing tool, whether pendulum or rod, are your own responses magnified, presented to you and to others in a clear form. You will discover that there is a direct relationship between your dowsing success and your clarity of mind. If your thoughts are muddled, confused or hazy, your dowsing results will be inconclusive. As you discover the value of clear thinking, lucid images and precise inner commands, you will learn something about yourself. Dowsing, like the theatre, demands a certain suspension of disbelief. This does not mean that you have to be committed to a belief in dowsing before you start. You can be convinced by your own experiences. However, if you deeply and firmly believe that dowsing cannot and indeed must not work, then it probably won't. You simply need to be open minded.

## LET'S GET STARTED

There are many devices for dowsing, from a simple needle suspended on a thread, to quite expensive commercial designs. Different tools suit different applications. Dowsing for water would

be difficult with a pendulum. Dowsing for a precise answer would be difficult using large and rather ungainly rods. Be prepared to have a go at different methods. They can all be fun.

# Pendulums

A pendulum is the most popular of all dowsing instruments. It is easily carried and always useful. It is important to remember from the outset, however, that a pendulum is no more than a weight on a thread. On its own the pendulum 'knows nothing'. It may, however, present what you 'know' in an accessible form. In my experience pendulums made from a wide variety of materials function perfectly effectively. You might like to try different materials for yourself. A brass plumb-bob has a nice feel to it. You don't have to save up for a commercial pendulum, a crystal, or even a plumb-bob – my personal favourite is a ring suspended from a thread. Some specialised pendulums are hollow so that a sample can be popped inside. But you do not have to wait. Most people wear a ring, so you can make a start with this. Always make sure you have a reasonable amount of thread. The length of cord may be significant in specialised work, especially if you are interested in setting up a particular experiment. Generally you will need enough cord to permit movement (25 cms). A long cord produces a slow, lazy rotation which takes a long time to stop and alter direction; too short a cord produces a rather frenetic movement. Feel free to experiment. Always bear in mind that the pendulum is simply an amplifier which serves to reproduce responses that exist below the threshold of consciousness. When we begin our journey into dowsing we will begin by establishing a good relationship between the different levels of the mind.

## The Long Pendulum

Tom Lethbridge was an intreprid dowser who pioneered the long pendulum. His researches led him to believe that different substances responded to different lengths of cord. If you want to try this, you will need a heavier weight for longer cords. You will also

need to wind long lengths of cord around a keeper of some kind. I
have found a builder's plumb-bob makes an excellent long
pendulum. It is well weighted and it is possible to simply mark off
the inches along the cord with felt tip pen. Having done this you are
ready to investigate whether different substances respond best to
different lengths of cord, and if so why. In Lethbridge's own words:
'Hold the pendulum over the sample substance keeping the ball
swinging gently backwards and forwards and unrolling the cord. At a
given point the pendulum will go into a circular motion. This is the
rate for that substance.' His lifelong experiments led him to tabulate
the following substances. The rate is the length of cord between the
top of the pendulum and the bottom of the windlass. It is important
to understand that according to Lethbridge this rate represented the
radius of the L-Field of the object as measured at ground level.

| Rate in inches | Responding substance |
| --- | --- |
| 5.5 | Phosphorous |
| 7 | Sulphur |
| 10 | Graphite |
| 12 | Carbon |
| 13 | Slate, concrete |
| 14 | Silica, glass flint |
| 15 | Glaze on pottery |
| 21.5 | Potassium |
| 22 | Silver, lead, calcium, sodium |
| 22.5 | Magnesium |
| 23.5 | Vegetable and mineral oils, amber |
| 24 | Diamond |
| 25 | Aluminium |
| 25.5 | Alcohol |
| 26.5 | Oxygen |
| 29 | Gold |
| 30 | Hydrogen |
| 30.5 | Copper and cobalt |
| 32 | Iron |
| 32.5 | Nickel |

Lethbridge's work is both fascinating and thought provoking. His findings also provide a starting point for personal experimentation. The reader is free to accept or actively challenge the hypothesis presented by Lethbridge.

## DIVINING RODS – THE L ROD

These too can be cheaply made. They are best suited to outside work, especially dowsing for water. Simply take a pair of wire coat hangers, cut away the hook. Next cut the remaining wire into a short arm of about 12 cms and a long arm of about 30 cms. Bend the wire until it forms an L shape. You will need to hold the rods by the short arm so that the long arm acts as a pointer and in a loosely clenched fist which will permit the rods to move. The L Rods work through a wrist response. The rods permit several responses. They can move to the left or to the right and can cross or be repelled from each other. You can also buy dowsing rods which are very like the homemade L Rods. These tend to have wooden sleeves around the short arm as handles and are generally quite inexpensive.

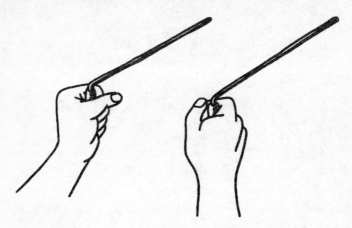

## NATURAL RODS – THE Y ROD

The traditional dowsing rod of course is the hazel twig. I have experimented with lots of woods and so far they have all

worked. I find that as these natural woods dry out they become less effective. Then it is time to look for another. The shape of the twig is important. You are looking for a Y shape. The wood needs to be springy and flexible. It can't be too thick or it won't respond. It shouldn't be too thin or it won't hold any tension. When you cut it, try to ensure that the two parts forming the 'handles' are of roughly equal length. The third section will form the pointer. It should not be cut too short.

I prefer using these natural tools when working outside. I like the fact that I am using a natural material. Personally I like the strong movements generated by this kind of rod. There is a genuine thrill as the rod suddenly seems to take on a life of its own as the pointer rotates, seemingly magnetised towards the ground or even pushed skywards. Working with this kind of rod gives a real sense of being in touch with natural energies. It is amazing to watch someone else working with this kind of rod. It is truly amazing to experience the sensation for yourself. Unlike either the pendulum or the L Rods, it

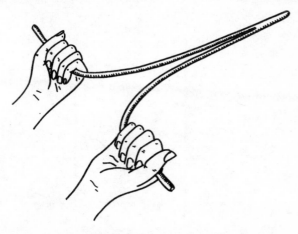

is hard to believe that you are generating this movement. The dowsing rod is probably magnifying a whole body response. Your entire body is aware, for instance, that water is near. This awareness is quite unconscious: the rod translates this surge of subtle energy into a visible response.

## The GEOLOGIST'S ROD

This is the rod designed by a team of Russian geologists. You will need about a metre of wire. A straightened-out coat hanger is perfectly serviceable as it gives you a reasonable length of wire. When you have straightened out your wire, make a small loop in the middle. Next make the sides by making two right-angled bends in the wire. Make the first bend by bending the wire towards you at about 10 cms from the loop. Make a second bend so that the ends of the rod are parallel to the loop. When the team used it they added an automatic rotation counter. If you take the trouble to make one of these, you will understand why it was thought desirable. The leading edge, with its loop, rotates completely and at speed. You need to hold the rod with arms outstretched in front of you. The movement here seems to come through the shoulders. This rod would probably be quite tiring to hold for a long period of time.

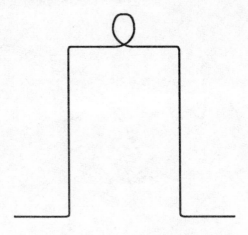

## The BOBBER

The bobber is probably the least used of all dowsing tools; however, it is simply made. The bobber is made from a long springy rod attached to a handle. It can be homemade using a cork for a handle and a long piece of brazing rod. You might feel that you want to add a little extra weight towards the end of the rod or you might try to work with a single flexible stem. You can use the bobber to move up and down to indicate 'yes' and side to side to indicate 'no'. The bobber is best suited to outside work.

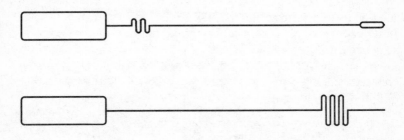

## The Aurameter

A good dowsing instrument has to be sensitive and flexible. Verne Cameron has developed an aurameter. It is very like the bobber in principle. It has a single arm which incorporates a coiled spring.

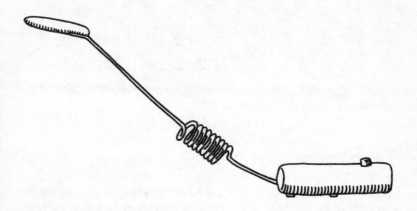

 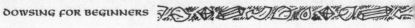

At the head of the pointer is a weight. I have found that natural Y Rods and L Rods are well suited to picking up auras.

New designs are always possible but I feel no-one has yet improved on the versatility of the pendulum or the satisfaction that you get from the natural rod. Dowsers often enjoy making a complicated looking rod. Guy Underwood designed his own rod: typically, few other people could operate it. We should not be bamboozled by expensive and complicated designs. The power to dowse can never be constructed. It lies in the operator not the instrument. It is clear that different dowsing instruments suit different situations and we will in time try them all.

| | Applications |
|---|---|
| **Short Pendulum** | Question and Answer technique, Direct Dowsing and Indirect Dowsing. |
| **Long Pendulum** | Assessing rates, locating rated substances. |
| **L Rod** | Locating underground features, pipes, water. |
| **Natural Rods** | Locating water, outside work. |
| **The Geologist's Rod** | Specially designed for locating mineral deposits. |
| **Bobbers** | Locating large energy fields, outside work, sacred sites. |
| **Aurameters** | Specially designed for working with auras. |

Always remember that no matter which instrument you are using, the only dowsing instrument is YOU.

# The techniques

*I discovered that everything has an energy field around it that looks somewhat like light from a candle. I also began to notice that*

*everything was connected by these energy fields, that no space existed without an energy field. Everything including me, was living in a sea of energy.*

Barbara Brennan, Hands of Light

Dowsing, like swimming, is a practical skill, so let's jump in at the deep end.

## EXERCISE 1 – THE ENERGIES OF LIFE

There is no doubt that a sensitivity to subtle energies can be developed. Dowsing depends upon our level of openness to the natural energies which surround us. This exercise establishes a sense of openness between the self and our surroundings. If you cannot complete this exercise outside in an open space, imagine that you are outside in a beautiful country spot.

Close your eyes. See yourself as a being surrounded by a rainbow light which extends in all directions around you like a living egg. Become aware of your surroundings: the trees, plants and grasses also emanate a gentle light. Do not try to see this light with your outer eye; simply become aware of it in your mind's eye. If trees are close together their lights will blend and mingle; if solitary, their lights will flare like a beacon against the sky. If you are beside water, imagine a luminescence hovering just above the surface. When you have become attuned to your surroundings, open your eyes and take a walk. As you walk, imagine that your own lights interact with all the natural lights around you. As you stand beneath a tree, your own light is temporarily taken into the greater light of the tree. As you walk past flowers and shrubs, tiny lights reach out to you in a wave as you pass. You may even reach out your hands to bathe in these delicate emanations. Even the ground on which you walk has an energy which interacts with your own. Know that these are the energies of life. Finish your exercise when you feel ready.

Welcome to the possibilities of dowsing!

We have already stressed that the power to dowse does not lie in the instrument but in the operator. In fact dowsing probably depends more on the ability to harmonise the conscious and

unconscious as aspects of the mind than on anything else. We have become over-reliant on the conscious mind. The following exercise serves to remind us that this reliance is essentially sterile. The conscious mind may appear formidable, yet it is only a part of the whole. Like an iceberg it rests upon the greater and unseen mass of the unconscious. No matter how big the iceberg appears, the vast bulk of it will always be hidden beneath the surface. Nevertheless, both the submerged part and the visible part are inseparably joined.

## EXERCISE 2 – THE ICEBERG

Close your eyes. See an image of an iceberg in your mind's eye. See that the conscious mind is only a part of the whole. Take your mind beneath the waters to the vast hidden bulk which will never surface. Dwell upon this relationship for a few moments. Give yourself permission to respond freely to the messages which arise from the deeper levels of consciousness. Simply affirm to yourself, 'I am open to the wisdom of my own subconscious mind.' Finish when you are ready.

You might be surprised that we have begun our dowsing work not by picking up a dowsing tool but with an exercise which is designed to open the mind and the senses. Always remember that the real dowsing tool is you. Moreover, dowsing is easily influenced by the mind set in which you as an individual live and operate. Now we will move onto a dowsing tool. We will start with the pendulum, which is highly versatile.

## EXERCISE 3 – SWING YOUR PENDULUM

Hold the thread between the thumb and the first finger. This gives a good sense of control. Now you are ready to start with some practical pendulum work. Mentally ask the pendulum to move in a clockwise direction. At the same time, visualise this happening in your mind's eye. Don't be surprised when the pendulum begins to pick up a nice steady clockwise gyration. After all, you have asked the deep levels of consciousness to assist you. The brain has

received a message and has transferred it to the muscles. Do not worry if you feel that you are doing it – you are. The pendulum has no power of its own.

When the pendulum has picked up a nice steady pace, stop it with your hand and be prepared to start again. This time mentally ask the pendulum to move in an anticlockwise direction. Once again, see the shape of the circle that you want in your mind's eye.

Practise these two actions until you are confident that you can produce these two movements at will. When you feel suitably pleased, if not surprised, move on to establish another movement, an oscillation back and forth. Ask the pendulum to move in a horizontal oscillation back and forth. Again, see the movement that you require in your mind.

---

See how the action of the pendulum is directly related to the clarity of your thought. Test your mental control through the following:

- Establish a clockwise gyration; stop the pendulum.
- Establish an anticlockwise gyration; stop the pendulum.
- Establish a clockwise gyration; establish an anticlockwise gyration.
- Establish an anticlockwise gyration; establish a clockwise gyration.
- Establish a horizontal oscillation; stop the pendulum.
- Can you establish any other regular movements under control?

---

If you really feel that nothing is happening, pay more attention to visualising the movement. Quite simply, the subconscious levels operate through images and symbols, not words. Don't be afraid to exert a little deliberate movement. This is not cheating. You need to become familiar with each different sensation. The movement merely amplifies the thought translated through the muscles. The mystery of dowsing does not lie in the movement of the pendulum, but in discovering just how much information is actually present and accessible at deeper levels of the mind.

You can have a lot of fun with this simple exercise. Before moving on, discover how long it takes to translate a thought into a movement. Is a clearly visualised thought more effective at producing a result than a command issued only through words?

## EXERCISE 4 – ESTABLISHING THE INNER CODE

The movements that you have established will form the basis of your personal code. You need to identify a particular movement with a particular meaning. You need to understand which direction means 'yes' and which direction means 'no' for you. Generally speaking a clockwise gyration indicates a positive response and an anticlockwise direction indicates a negative response. There is, however, no hard and fast rule, and it may have something to do with the handedness of the operator. You therefore need to establish your own code. In addition to the positive or negative response, you can utilise a third response which can be linked to a simple answer, such as, 'don't know'.

Establish your inner code by asking a series of unequivocal questions:

- Am I a woman?
- Am I a man?
- Is my name . . . ?
- Is today . . . ?
- Is my birthday on . . . ?

Make up some unequivocal question of your own.

When you expect an affirmative answer, programme the pendulum to respond in the way in which you wish it to continue to answer 'yes' for you in the future. Do the same when you anticipate a negative answer. You need to establish this code for yourself. You need to be confident that this code is deeply built into your psyche. So practise every day until you always get the appropriate responses for 'yes' and 'no'. At this stage stick to questions which give definite answers. Do not proceed until you are truly confident that you have established your own inner code. When you are confident that your code is consistent, you can begin to apply your pendulum work to real life situations. When using the pendulum to answer questions, you will soon discover that ambiguous questions give ambiguous answers. Confusion in the mind will certainly result in confusion through the pendulum. Preparing your questions in advance provides a valuable lesson in logical thinking, as you will soon discover if you ask an open-ended question.

Before you move on, check that you have answered the following:

- How does your pendulum show you 'yes'?
- How does your pendulum show you 'no'?

If you want to work regularly with another dowsing instrument, you will, as a preliminary exercise, need to establish a code which suits the instrument.

## TECHNIQUE 1 — QUESTION AND ANSWER

When you are confident that your inner code is established, you are ready to apply this technique in appropriate situations for yourself. Remember the success of this technique will depend totally on the clarity of your own thoughts. A muddled question will give an indefinite answer. You may find it useful to hear yourself saying the words to your question in your mind. You may ask questions to which you can expect a positive, negative or a neutral answer. The question and answer technique underpins indirect dowsing when we apply a series of questions to a list, a series of options, or to a sample from someone.

## TECHNIQUE 2 — DIRECT DOWSING

There are many situations in which questions have little relevance. The pendulum acts as an extension of your own energy field which is constantly interacting with the energy field around you. This process happens subliminally. However, it can be quite fascinating to permit the pendulum to amplify these responses for you. This requires a slightly different mind set. You need to have a clear, open and passive mind. You should have no expectations. You do not know how the pendulum will react across a range of substances, so this exercise is pure experiment.

## TECHNIQUE 3 — SEARCHING

This is also a form of direct dowsing. The difference is that you do not know where you will locate the energy field that you want to isolate from the surroundings. Lethbridge reported some remarkable successes when he used dowsing techniques to search for buried objects. He selected the length of cord that was appropriate for the substance he was looking for and simply walked across the area of search. When you are searching for something, you need to be mentally attuned to it. If you are actively searching for water, you need to make this clear to the subconscious. If you are searching for electricity cables, you need to make this clear too. Use a positive and clear statement of intent, create a clear target in your mind. Affirm, 'I am searching for water', or anything else for that matter.

## TECHNIQUE 4 — INDIRECT DOWSING

You may not always have the object in front of you. It may not be practical to dowse directly. For instance, if you are looking for a suitable remedy from a large group, you will not want to dowse each item individually. You need to use an intermediary. This can take many forms. It might be appropriate to construct a list. In some instances it is appropriate to use a sample. This is called a witness, as it represents the subject of the enquiry. It is also possible to dowse at a distance using a map as a representation.

These four techniques will provide you with a wide range of possibilities.

# DOWSING FOR WATER

*Can someone walking along holding a forked stick – a dowser – really find mineral veins, water or hidden things underground?*
Tom Williamson, Dowsing: New Light on an Ancient Art

It is likely that dowsing for water dates back to the dawn of time. However, the first water dowser to become famous was Martine de Bertereau, a sixteenth century gentlewoman, who was married to Jean de Chastelet, Baron de Beausoleill et d'Auffenbach. He was the leading mining expert of his day and held the post as Commissioner General of the three Chambers of Mines of Hungary. He also worked for the Austrian Archduke Leopold, as director for mines on the Tyrol and Trent, and as mining adviser to successive Dukes of Bavaria. Martine de Bertereau was a most unusual woman, and she accompanied her husband on his many underground explorations. She learned dowsing from the miners of Trent and Tyrol and simply applied what she had learned from them. Her natural interest and enthusiasm rendered her an extremely gifted and accurate dowser. She discovered mineral springs in the town of Chateau-Thierry. In 1626 she and her husband were commissioned to advise the state on possible mining ventures in France. In her report she listed lead, silver and tin deposits in Brittany, amethyst mines in the Auvergne, yellow amber in Picardy, and lead and silver in Provence. Their success brought inevitable jealousy. Their enemies accused them of using diabolical magic. In 1627 the Provost of the Duke of Brittany confiscated all their instruments, mineral specimens, reports and maps. On this occasion the Baron successfully defended himself in court against the charges. However, the Baron underestimated the changing climate in which he was working.

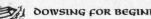 

In the 1640s the Baroness published *La Restitution de Pluton*. Its dedication to Cardinal Richelieu was to prove a fatal mistake. The Baroness openly asked the Cardinal to develop the mineral wealth of France.

> *France and the French ask you for mines,*
> *Gold, silver, azure, lodestones, calamines,*
> *They are treasures hidden by the spirit of God*
> *If you authorise what I propose*
> *You will see, Monseigneur, without metamorphose,*
> *France will truly become a 'Riche-Lieu'.*

The Baroness spoke openly about dowsing as a means of locating mineral wealth. 'There are seven dowsing rods of which the knowledge and practice is most necessary, which the ancients used to discover from the surface, metals hidden in the depths. And also to discover sources of water.' This innocence and naiveté was an open invitation for persecution. It was not a safe time to employ the dowsing rod. Cardinal Richelieu had them arrested and placed in separate prisons, where they eventually died. Two of their four children were also arrested. Fortunately, we may dowse with impunity.

Locating water is of course a most valuable faculty, as some adventurous companies discovered to their benefit. The Bristol born stonemason William Scott Lawrence located wells in the west country for many noted Victorian establishments, including the Bristol Wagon Works and Tiverton Town Council. John Mullins became the most famous Victorian dowser of all. Among his many achievements was the finding of water for a firm of bacon curers in Waterford, Ireland in 1887. He located a perfect and plentiful supply using only his hazel rod. The company had previously sunk three expensive bore holes with no success. In total Mullins was credited with finding some 5,000 sources of water in the British Isles. He eventually ran his own well-sinking business on a money-back basis. His undoubted success did a great deal to give dowsing a respectable and solid image. His common sense and success proved that water divining could be treated as a professional skill, rather than an arcane and diabolic conspiracy.

Germany too saw the economic advantages of successful dowsing. It was the German military who employed a series of officer-dowsers to find water both at home and in their colonies. In the same tradition of efficiency and expertise, the GTZ, a technical aid agency working in the Third World, employs the skills of water diviners to locate pure sources of water for villages. The team leader, Hans Schroter, has been employed to find water in Sri Lanka, the Dominican Republic, Yemen, Cape Verde and Namibia. I have never been employed to find water but I've had a lot of fun finding it for myself.

I first taught myself to dowse for water while on holiday in France. We stayed at a cottage in the Dordogne. The cottage belonged to a farmer who also owned the adjacent field. I was bored. The days were long. There was little to do except pick vegetables from the patch, prepare lunch and sunbathe and read. One morning while taking a stroll I decided to try my luck at water divining. I cut a suitable shape from the hedge and then wondered what to do with it. I held the two stems loosely, one in each hand, and began to walk around the edge of the field following the line of the hedge. Nothing happened for a while. I then began to follow the edge of the field parallel to the house and the twig began to pull. It was a very strange sensation. It felt as if it had become magnetised. A few more steps and the end of the twig was pointing directly down into the ground. I was fascinated. I took several steps backwards and then moved slowly forwards. No matter how many times I repeated this, the twig reacted in the same way and at the same place. I spent a good part of the morning just walking around the field. There wasn't much happening except at one spot. I traced the outline of this area of activity by approaching from various directions. The reactions indicated a block of activity. As I learned later, it was of course the underground cesspit. My holiday was enlivened by discovering the routes of piping beneath the quarry tiled floor. Since then I have experimented with different types of twig, different sizes of twig, with metal coat hangers and professional rods. I have to say I still prefer the living wood. There is nothing to match the sensation as the twig begins to pull and revolve between your hands.

Two thirds of the planet consists of water. Our bodies have a high

water content, so is it really any surprise that we should be able to detect water, the most essential requirement for life? As with all dowsing, successful location depends upon tuning the sensitivities to a particular wavelength.

If you are planning to locate water anywhere outside, everything else in the immediate environment will also be giving out its own energy. The grass, trees, plants, living creatures, rocks and soil will also be radiating their own life force which presumably you do not need. By focusing on what you are actively looking for, you will be able to screen out everything else.

## EXERCISE 1 – WATER, WATER, EVERYWHERE

To really sensitise yourself to water, employ your imaginative powers as fully as you can. Imagine that you are really thirsty. How can you make this feeling real in your imagination? Perhaps you have just been out for a long run. Perhaps you have just been sunbathing and you really need a drink of cool clear water. If you have a taste for the dramatic, perhaps you are lost in the desert, desperate for water to save your life. Having made yourself really thirsty, imagine the taste and feel of fresh water on your skin and in your mouth. Hear the sound of running water nearby. You are so looking forward to splashing water over your face. You just have to find the water that you need. It isn't far away. Of course at home water is never far away, so you can begin your experiments with water immediately.

## EXERCISE 2 – FINDING WATER

### TECHNIQUE: DIRECT DOWSING

Take three containers of different sizes, perhaps a cup, a small bowl and a large bowl. Take your pendulum and hold it over the surface of the water in each container. Tell yourself 'I'm searching for water', and remind yourself just how much you are looking forward to finding it. Although in this instance you are hardly

'looking' for water, use this opportunity to connect your mental desire with the response of the pendulum. It is this ability to connect mind and body which lies behind all dowsing success. When your pendulum starts to move over the water, note its direction. Is there a relationship between the size of the circle described by the pendulum and the circumference of the container?

When you are confident that dowsing over water, even in small quantities, gives you a reaction, change the tool for the job and see what reaction you get using a natural rod cut from a brush or tree, and also from L Rods. Compare your reactions:

- Do you prefer the strong and steady gyration of the pendulum to the movement generated by the rods?

- What happens when you use a natural rod?

- Does the pointer swing up for you or down?

- Does it move when directly over the water, or at a point before or slightly after the water?

- What happens when you approach the water with L Rods? Do they cross or swing apart?

- How close are you to the water before you get a response from the rods?

- Of the three dowsing tools which do you prefer in the given situation?

If you really want to develop your sensitivity to water, get into the habit of dowsing water whenever possible. Take samples when visiting. Water varies a great deal from district to district. Dowsing samples of tapwater can be highly instructive. You may soon stop drinking it.

## EXERCISE 3 – WHAT'S IN TAP WATER?

### TECHNIQUE: DIRECT DOWSING

Compare water from your own tap with a sample of bottled spring water. You may need to refine your thoughts here. If you simply

state, 'I'm searching for water', you will surely get a positive response in both instances. You will need to decide precisely what you want to know from each sample. Use the pendulum to dowse directly. When the gyration is established, pose your question, 'Is this water pure enough to drink?'

You may get quite a different response from each sample. I was quite surprised recently when a friend demonstrated a water purification system to me. I asked her to take a sample from both the unfiltered tap and from the filtered water. While my back was turned she lay out the two samples in identical white cups. When I dowsed them with the intention of assessing purity, one sample gave a clockwise reaction, which I identify as a normal healthy response. The second sample gave the same reaction that I get from unhealthy plants and areas of sickness, a straight horizontal movement. You may be more fortunate. Perhaps your tap water will pass the purity test.

I find that a clear mental question is sufficient to elicit a response. However, a simple 'yes' or 'no' may be insufficient if we are seeking further information. We may want to ask further questions. If for instance we have established that the water is not pure enough to drink we may want to discover in what way the water is impure.

# The Mager Rosette

### Technique: Indirect Dowsing

The Frenchman Henri Mager also wrestled with the same problem and came up with his own solution. He codified the possible responses and presented them in visual form. The Mager Rosette is a disk divided into eight equal sections coloured violet, blue, green, yellow, red, grey, black and white. The disk is usually about ten centimetres in diameter. This is merely for convenience.

The colours of the Mager Rosette are:

- Violet – absolutely pure

- Blue – normal drinking water

- Green – mineralisation present
- Yellow – hard water salts present
- Red – iron content
- Grey – polluted water probably with lead
- Black – black streams bad for health
- White – healing water

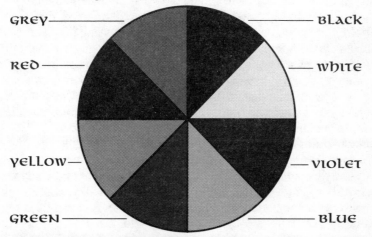

The disk merely serves as a shorthand between your question and the answer that you are looking for. There is nothing magical about the device itself. However, it is easy to make and to experiment with. When using the rosette, hold the colour that you have selected between the finger and thumb of one hand while holding the pendulum in the other.

As you delve more deeply into dowsing you will discover it is truly a pastime where the individual can be king. Practice makes perfect. If something works for you, then it works, since we are each quite different in sensitivity, temperament and mental outlook. We should be used to different operations suiting different people. I have to admit being a little surprised to read that one very experienced dowser recommended making a Mager Rosette some 2 to 3 ft in diameter. He therefore applied this quite differently from the small

hand-held version. This dowser laid the rosette on the ground with the violet segment facing north. He then paced around it holding the divining rod. He experienced a lift of the rod at the four cardinal points corresponding to the violet, green, red and black segments on the rosette. These reactions are then used as a test for determining affinities between various metals and colours. When an affinity is discovered between a metal and a colour, such as silver, copper or lead, the dowsing rod will be seen to lift at the four quarters. Where no affinity is present, there will be no reaction. When an affinity between a substance and a colour has been discovered, the appropriate colour may then be used when dowsing for a particular substance. This somewhat cumbersome process may serve to link a wide range of substances. It may also offer a broad colour code. For instance a given substance may react best to the cusps between colour segments, red-grey, green-yellow for instance. The relevant colour may be painted onto a rod, made up as a coloured sample or simply held in the mind. This rather complicated procedure demonstrates a very simple principle: dowsing works best through the establishment and development of a personal inner code. Finding this personal code is a matter of experiment and discovery. It is also a matter of great fun. An internal colour code might work very well for someone with a good visual sense. An artist used to working with many colours might easily visualise a deep violet or a greeny yellow. Conversely, someone unused to a wide range of colour might be unable to operate through an internal colour code.

The Mager Rosette is clearly only an external coding device. Other codes are of course possible. Take a bold step and invent your own. The key to establishing a code that others might also use is to choose symbols that are easily understood at a glance. I have elaborated on Mager's original code with everyday symbols. Do the same: always feel free to experiment, to refine and develop any idea given to you. Here are some suggestions:

- Violet – absolutely pure – a star
- Blue – normal drinking water – a chalice
- Green – mineralisation present – rocks
- Yellow – hard water salts present – a block of salt

- Red – iron content – a nail
- Grey – polluted water probably with lead – a coffin, or a ghostly phantom
- Black – black streams bad for health – a skull and crossbones

A code based on astrological symbols might work just as well:

- Moon – healing waters
- Mars – iron
- Venus – copper
- Saturn – lead, polluted waters
- Jupiter – tin
- Sun – absolutely pure, life giving
- Pluto – black streams, bad for health
- Earth – mineralisation present

## EXERCISE 4 – COLOURS

Make a traditional Mager Rosette.

## EXERCISE 5 – SYMBOLS

Make a non traditional Rosette using symbols of your own choice.

## EXERCISE 6 – SOLUTIONS

### TECHNIQUE: DIRECT DOWSING

Experiment with picking up solid material. If you hope to attune yourself to metals dissolved in water, you can develop your sensitivity by dowsing specifically for these metals. You have already dowsed for water. Do expect a different reaction if you place

a piece of metal in water. Try dowsing for a copper coin or an iron nail in a bowl of water:

- What reaction do you get from the pendulum when the water contains a metal sample?

- Do you get the same reaction regardless of the metal sample that you try?

- Is there any way of detecting the presence of a known metal in the water? Try a long pendulum set to Lethbridge's rate.

Impure water contains high levels of solid material dissolved in solution. Our natural curiosity should lead us to explore the dowsed responses of known solutions:

- Add salt to water, what reaction do you get as the solution is increased in strength?

- Add sugar to water, what reaction do you get as the solution gets stronger?

- Add a drop from a Bach flower remedy. What reaction do you get if you make the solution stronger?

- Now try dowsing each of the solutions with your Mager Rosette in your other hand. Again experiment with a traditional design and your own homemade design.

# Water Divining

*What matters most is the particular method you have in your mind.*
Arthur Bailey, Dowsing for Health

You will have discovered that water, even in small quantities produces a very powerful reaction. Most dowsers favour a rod of some kind for actual water divining. You have the opportunity to practise with both the L Rods and a natural rod. It is quite likely that you will develop a preference for one kind of rod.

Dowsing is a totally individual domain. There are hardly any hard

and fast rules, only suggestions and possibilities. When researching
the various ways of determining the depth and flow of a stream, I
was amazed by the variety, and at times quite put off by the
complexity of various idiosyncratic approaches. The following
practices can be used or adapted as required. Always feel free to
experiment.

## TO DETERMINE THE COURSE OF A STREAM

Walk across the land with the dowsing twig under tension.
When you get a reaction, mark the spot with a peg. It might
be helpful to work with a friend. Continue walking until you get
another reaction. Place another mark here. Move along the field and
continue the operation putting down markers as you go. However,
these markers do not represent the width of the stream as might
commonly be expected. Dowsers refer to these boundaries as lines
of influence. The distance between them is an expression of depth at
which the stream will be found. The wider the distance between the
markers, the deeper the stream. The actual water will be located at
the midpoint of the two boundary markers.

## TO DETERMINE THE FLOW OF A STREAM

This is the procedure followed by Ralph Whitlock, a very
experienced water diviner. Stand in the middle of the zone you
have marked. Hold the twig in position and walk slowly along the
centre of the band. If you are walking against the flow of the stream
the pointer will lift; if you are walking with it, the pointer will dip.

## TO DETERMINE THE DEPTH AT WHICH WATER WILL BE LOCATED

Ralph Whitlock suggests the following:

Stand at a point which has been established as being over the
centre of the subterranean stream. Hold the pendulum between

thumb and finger of an outstretched hand: soon the pendulum will start to oscillate, which is the signal to start counting aloud at a steady rate. Presently the number of oscillations will quite suddenly switch gyrations. Make a note of the number reached in the counting when this happens.

A second method uses a forked twig. Stand at the centre of the stream band and grasp the arms of the twig in the approved manner. When the pointer jerks upwards, which will happen almost immediately, release one arm of the fork then grasp again and start counting. When the pointer lifts again, the number of reactions will be the same as discovered by the pendulum, and will indicate the depth below the surface at which the water exists.

A third method of determining the depth at which water will be located is called the Bishop's Rule. According to this formula, 'distance out equals distance down'. Dowsers are familiar with this

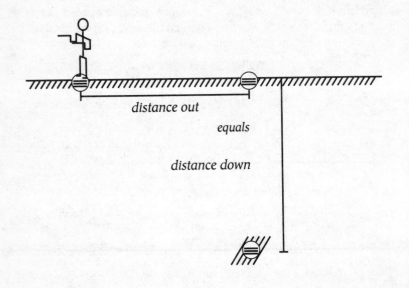

distance out

equals

distance down

equation. The Bishop's Rule expresses a relationship which is commonly attested to be accurate. It seems that the depth at which the stream is located underground is matched on either side by boundaries which exist at an equivalent distance from each side of it. Mark a point above a pipe or stream, then walk at right angles to the flow for a new response. The distance between the first point above the stream or pipe and the second point is equivalent to the distance down. Hence 'distance out = distance down'. Finally, the Point–Depth method involves driving a rod into the ground at the centre of the stream, walking in a circle around it, and recording the number of circles completed before the rod lifts. The variety of these methods again highlights the view that there are no hard and fast rules. If you set the rules, they will work for you. Be bold and devise your own system. You will be much happier with it in the long run.

- How do you think you might use a dowsing rod to show you the direction of flow?

- How do you think you might assess the depth at which water will be located?

You will need to incorporate a counting system of some kind.

# Sacred wells

*We found that a number of holy wells we checked yielded higher than the background radiation at water surface – considerably higher in some cases.*

Paul Devereux, Earth Memory

The Folk tradition of the British Isles has many stories to tell of sacred springs and wells. The most famous well of all is probably the Chalice Well at Glastonbury. Keith Paull, an amateur and enthusiastic dowser, offers us some fascinating insights into the waters at Glastonbury. The article first appeared in *Quest* no. 95. It is reprinted here with the author's kind permission.

# POTENCY INCREASE IN SACRED SPRING WATERS

'For many years I have been interested in the dowsing reactions obtainable at ancient sites, sacred springs and the like. I have tried to study these effects with as much objectivity as is possible in such a subjective field and I leave it to others to determine to what uses, if any these observations may be put. Although I have had a number of successes in dowsing, including work in the field of noxious energy location and its neutralisation I would certainly not claim the results of my experiments to be either definitive or even applicable to work performed by others particularly in the field of healing.

I offer the following in quite the opposite manner to that of the many self-professed experts, who after five minutes pendulum waggling and with little or no serious study, proclaims that his or her spirit guide/entity from another planet/astral guardian or what have you has told them, that theirs is the only correct technique and all else is the work of mischievous spirits/enemy/aliens/demons or such like.

I have noticed that when dowsing with the pendulum over a sample of water from a sacred spring such as the Glastonbury Chalice Well and the mental request "Please indicate the signature of this water" formulated, the pendulum swings in a manner unique to that particular sample. In the case of Chalice Well water, for me the pendulum rotates alternately four revolutions clockwise, then four counter-clockwise whilst with other samples there appear other patterns of swing, some asymmetric left and right rotations and others composed of combinations of rotation and oscillation.

As a method of measuring the intensity of the dowsing reaction, if I already have a value which I might use as a reference, I simply count up or down, my rod twitching or the pendulum changing direction when I come to the required multiplier or divisor. My mental question might therefore be:

"Does this sample have a greater strength than the previous one?" to which I get a conventional yes/no reaction. Assuming the answer

is positive then the next instruction would be: "Please indicate when I come to the correct multiplier." Then I would start counting. If counting "Times One", "Times Two", etc. . . . threatens to go on forever try "Times Ten", "Times Twenty" and so on.

For many years I have been interested in the work of several researchers, notably that of Lethbridge and of Fiddler, and it occurred to me that perhaps it might be possible to combine some of the results they have recorded, particularly in the fields of transferring or inducing a dowsable effect in a previously inert medium. My first experiment consisted of attempting to transfer the dowsing signal obtained from a piece of stone taken from a crop circle and replicate it in a dozen other stones in this case sea-worn quartz pebbles picked up on a beach. I placed the pebbles together with the mother-stone in a glass bowl of water and left them for a period of five days, at the end of which the dowsing signal from each specimen, including the original stone, was identical. What was completely unexpected was that the water in the bowl had also taken on exactly the same characteristics! This leads me to wonder if the dowsing signatures of various sacred springs derive not directly from the water but from something in the rock strata through which it flows.

As an engineer and a scientist well acquainted with the laws of conservation of energy it seemed a little unreasonable to finish up with twelve extra stones and two pints of water exactly identical with the mother-stone prior to the experiment! Then I remembered the principles of homoeopathic potency, could this possibly be involved? A healer friend who has worked for several years with healing pads consisting of a wad of cotton wool 'charged' with healing energy has frequently demonstrated that a pad may be divided into many smaller pads for distribution to other patients without losing any of its effectiveness. Might it be that sacred spring water could be diluted with "ordinary" water in exactly the same manner, transferring and maybe intensifying both its dowsable effect and any other properties it may have? Experiments using the previously described measuring technique suggest that this is indeed possible, in the case of Chalice Well water the efficacy rising to a maximum at a potency of five, cutting off drastically thereafter.

Many people believe it would be wonderful to be able to bathe in the water from a sacred well, so to obtain a working potency of five, that is a dilution of 1/100,000 in your tub I suggest the following procedure might well be followed. Half fill a one litre bottle with ordinary tap water and add to it 2 teaspoons of sacred spring water. Then shake the mixture as violently as possible for a couple of minutes. This gives a mixture with a potency of 2 and becomes your working solution. When starting to run the bath add ONE EGG-CUP of the working solution to the stream of water coming from the tap thus giving it the maximum chance to mingle and, for a normal bath of 50 litres you will have an average dilution of 1 in 100,000. If you are a dowser yourself and are using water from some other source it would make sense to check for yourself the required potency using the technique suggested above. I hope the preceding notes will be of interest and provoke further thought and experiment, but above all do not just follow my suggestions as if they are the utterances of some oracle guided by the gods. THEY ARE NOT!'

The preceding article is especially interesting. It emphasises personal experiment and discovery while debunking supposedly accepted wisdom. This is a wonderfully healthy attitude which I wholeheartedly support. In dowsing you must find what works best for you. This may or may not be the same approach as that proven by someone else. Second-hand experience may be a good teacher. But firsthand experience is the best teacher. The work suggested in the article is new to me and all the more exciting for that. When I have the opportunity to dowse reputedly sacred water I most certainly will try this approach. I look forward to the results. We can all take a leaf out of this particular book of wisdom. Always remember, keep it practical, keep it simple and you won't go far wrong.

# 3 ÐOWSING FOR HEALTH

*Once the field of medicines and other therapies is entered, there is a completely new field to be considered.*

Arthur Bailey, Dowsing for Health

Health and well-being are of great importance to everyone. We know that our physical health is closely connected to our emotional and mental states. Long-term stress sets up patterns which are reflected at physical levels of being. We carry our emotional lives through our bodies. We bear heavy burdens on stooped shoulders. We carry inner tensions in tight muscles. Body language acts like a mirror for our inner life. Physical health cannot be separated from the well-being of the mind and the well-being of the emotions. What can we learn about ourselves through dowsing? We have talked about the relationship between the physical form and its energy field, so let's investigate this in relation to our own physical well-being.

Let us jump in at the deep end and begin with a practical experiment. When you have discovered your own energy field, you will be that much better equipped to interact with other energy fields.

## EXERCISE 1 – FINDING THE ENERGY FIELD

Place your hands so that the palms are facing one another but do not touch. Begin to move your hands in a bouncing movement towards and then apart from one another. You might already begin

to feel something at this point. When the two palm centres interact, you will feel what people invariably describe as 'magnetism'. This feeling is unmistakable. It is quite different from the experience of general body heat. If you do not experience this particular sensation realign the palms in relation to each other. There is a minor chakra point in the centre of each palm. These need to 'lock' into each other. When you discover this sensation, you can begin to experiment. Move your hands a little further apart. Eventually the magnetic contact will be broken.

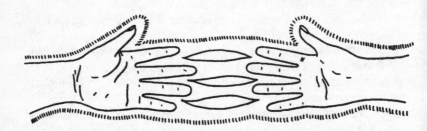

## EXERCISE 2 – WHITE LIGHT

When you have confidently experienced the feeling of magnetism between your hands, you can intensify the experience. Hold the palms together as before. But this time pay attention to your breathing pattern. Breath in deeply and slowly. Imagine white light pouring in through the top of your head. On the out breath, visualise white light pouring out from each palm. Repeat this simple pattern. Assess the difference. Did the magnetic field feel stronger on each out breath? Did you have any difficulty holding the image of the white light? If so, practise this exercise until you can really feel the difference.

## EXERCISE 3 – FINGERTIPS

Take time to increase your sensitivity even further. Dowsing is about sensitivity to subtle energies. Close your eyes. Experiment by using only the fingertips of one hand against the palm of the other hand. What can you feel through the palm of one hand as you move the fingers, or just a single finger of the other hand, close to it? Assess your reactions. Is the palm of one more sensitive than the palm of the other? Does this bear any relationship to whether you are right or left handed?

## EXERCISE 4 – SHARING ENERGY

You can also try this with another person. Sit facing each other. Let one person hold out both palms facing upwards. Let the other person hold out both palms facing downwards. Energy can flow from one person to another. Let the person with hands facing up be the receiver. Let the person with palms down be the sender. Let the sender employ the same technique as earlier described. Imagine white light descending into you and flowing out through your palms into the outstretched palms of your friend. Let the receiver be as sensitive as possible to any sensations that take place through the palms. Change places. What did you discover? Is the distance between the hands of the two people important? Did you both feel the magnetic force between you? How far did you stretch your hands away from each other before the contact was broken? Did you sense any differences between sending and receiving? Did you find one easier than the other? If you are sending energy it is likely that your hands will suddenly become very cold. If you are receiving energy from another person your hands will conversely become warm.

These exercises are good preparation for dowsing. The next time you are ready to try a dowsing experiment, try it twice. First proceed without any preparation. Then prepare yourself for just a few moments by utilising the image of the white light descending through you. Assess whether this preparation improved your dowsing ability. When you have discovered your own energy field,

you will feel confident about working with someone else. Of course you have been working simply through your hands. Now you might like to work through a pendulum.

## EXERCISE 5 – CIRCLES AND LINES

### TECHNIQUE: DIRECT DOWSING

Ask your friend to hold out one hand, it does not matter which hand you begin with. Hold your pendulum over the palm of the hand. When the pendulum has established a clear rotation, ask your friend to change hands. You do not have to stop the pendulum; simply place the other hand beneath it. What do you discover? Did the pendulum move in an oscillation or a gyration? Did it move in the same direction over each hand? If your friend is willing, continue the experiment. Perhaps your friend will lay out flat. Dowse the right side of the body, starting at the feet working up the leg, moving up over the abdomen, chest and then down over the arm and into the hand. Repeat your dowsing down the left side of the body in the same way. What do you discover? Record your findings by drawing a rough diagram. Perhaps you and your friend might swap roles. Prepare another diagram. What have you discovered? You might also take a reading from the back of the body and compare it with that taken from the front. It is most likely that you will record a series of opposing circular gyrations as you dowse over the left and right sides of the body. The body has several polarised energy systems. This left–right polarity is a major axis.

If you locate areas where the pendulum oscillates instead, stop and ask your friend if this area is related to injury or damage. If you have the opportunity to work in this way with a large number of people, you will be surprised to discover how old injuries leave a trace for a long time.

- What have you learned about the body's polarity through the pendulum?

- What have you discovered about healthy normal tissue through the pendulum?

- What have you discovered about damaged tissue through the pendulum?

I remember running a dowsing check over a very sceptical friend. He was young and looked very healthy. I was surprised when the pendulum began to oscillate over one shoulder. I stopped at this point and asked him about his shoulder, which he assured me was perfectly normal. However, after a few moments, he recalled a skiing injury which had taken place a year previously. It was clear from the reading that this area was still not fully healed. I was at first quite amazed to locate old injuries but it has happened on so many occasions that I am no longer surprised when it happens.

You may use this simple application as a means of learning about your own healing process. When you have detected the difference between healthy and non-healthy tissue, you may observe as one state moves into the other. You may monitor your own return to health from common complaints such as flu, chesty colds, sprains and stomach upsets. When you are ill, simply get used to registering its extent on a daily basis. You will learn a great deal about yourself. You may also use this to register the impact of interventions, especially those which work directly upon the energy systems.

An experienced and competent dowser might use the pendulum as a means of checking the functions of individual organs. This is an advanced and specialised use of dowsing. In principle the health of any organ can be checked individually. However, you should first be fully acquainted with the principles of anatomy. The more you know about the body, the more you will be able to apply dowsing skills in the service of healing. Dowsing in this way should be used as an adjunct to existing medical knowledge, not as a substitute. However, there is no reason why you should not practise on yourself. Pendulum work is of course perfectly harmless and you might learn something.

I have always used every episode of personal illness as an opportunity to learn more about the subtle ways in which the body functions. When I first went for acupuncture treatment, I monitored my own energy both before and after treatment. I simply laid out flat and observed the reaction of the pendulum over the front of the

body. Before treatment the pendulum showed strong oscillation over the abdomen. At the time the treatment affected me very powerfully. I had to make a long drive home and it was a difficult journey. I simply felt 'spaced out'. I was curious enough to test my own reaction again before pulling up a cover and falling asleep. The pendulum now showed a tremendous linear swing right up the front of the body. I fell straight into a long and deep sleep. When I awoke I tested myself again. The linear swing had now been replaced by circular gyrations. Indeed one treatment cured the physical problems that I had suffered.

We can also apply what we know about the energy field to animals. On another occasion my cat went missing. She was eventually found sheltering in the basement. It was clear something was very wrong with her. At first we thought she had been involved in a road accident but it soon became clear that she had in fact been poisoned, probably by eating something infected with a garden weed killer. She lay listlessly in a box taking only water. I held a pendulum over her. The results were entirely negative. The situation looked pretty hopeless. I tested her again after three days. She looked exactly the same to me. However, the pendulum showed me a positive reaction which then became negative as I moved along the length of her body. Healing had taken place. This was an encouraging sign and I felt confident that she would make a recovery, which indeed she did.

# Dowsing and food

Who can deny the importance of good food for good health? Direct dowsing can provide an instant picture of the vitality offered by different foods. There is no doubt that eating habits have changed considerably in recent years. Perhaps the trade between nutritional value and convenience has gone too far.

## EXERCISE 6 – YOU ARE WHAT YOU EAT

### TECHNIQUE: DIRECT DOWSING

Make a wide selection using meat, vegetables, fruit, grains, etc. Hold your pendulum over each sample in turn. Record your results. When testing, always make sure that each sample is kept physically separate from the next one. Take a selection of foods which fall into different categories. Test them with your pendulum. What can you learn from your samples? The question that you frame will of course determine the answer that you get. 'Is this OK for me to eat?' is not the same as 'Should I eat this?' 'Will I gain nutritionally from this food?' is not the same as 'Will I enjoy eating this?' 'Is this food uncontaminated?' is not the same as 'Does this food possess life force?' You can ask all of these questions of each foodstuff if you wish. You may be surprised at the answers. You can extend your experiment by comparing different ways of presenting the same product. Using your pendulum,

- Compare fresh meat with frozen meat.

- Compare a battery egg with a free range egg.

- Compare white bread with brown bread.

- Compare fresh vegetables with frozen vegetables.

- Test the drinks available for children.

Compare squashes, concentrates, freshly squeezed juices, canned drinks, milk.

## EXERCISE 7 – LIKES AND DISLIKES

### TECHNIQUE: DIRECT DOWSING

Everyone is an individual. We do not all respond in the same way to either food or medicine. Bitter experience has shown me that I am allergic to several commonplace medicines. Knowing this,

means that I always refuse them. In this instance forewarned is truly forearmed. Discovering an allergy can be a very slow and often unpleasant process. In my case one common medicine makes me very sick, another medicine makes me pass out almost instantly. Locating a food allergy can also be a very slow process as it is usual to exclude a suspected food from the diet and then introduce it in order to observe the results of eating it. Dowsing can provide a quick and reliable allergy test. When you are confident you may be happy to be guided entirely by the result. If you lack this confidence perhaps use what you discover through dowsing to support an allergy testing programme.

When my daughter was about seven her behaviour became rather erratic. I began to suspect that food allergies might be involved after a particular episode related to drinking blackcurrant juice. A friend in similar circumstances had arranged allergy testing at the local hospital. However, she had to wait a long time. At that time I had never used a pendulum in this way before. My daughter, who was already quite good at water divining, was interested to give it a go. We laid out samples of everyday foods. I held the pendulum and she held my hand. We moved from sample to sample asking both aloud and mentally, 'Is this good for Eve to eat?' The results were quite fascinating. The pendulum changed from negative to positive as we passed along the line. When she let go of my hand, a negative response changed to a positive one. When she held my hand again the pendulum resumed its negative response. According to our reading, oranges were good for her, orange juice other than freshly squeezed was bad for her. Blackcurrant juice was disastrous. Milk was OK. Certain biscuits were good, others were not. Most vegetables were OK, with the exception of sweetcorn. Certain types of sweets especially the jelly type were not good, others were OK. She was relieved that crisps were OK, I was surprised. We reorganised her diet. She had instructions not to take offending drinks at other people's houses or social events. Her behaviour stabilised and we did not have to go on a waiting list at the local hospital.

Initially it is a good idea to test a sample of the actual substance that you want to test. You can do this directly by holding a

pendulum over the food. Focus your mind and pose the question, 'Is this food good for me?' You can try another method of allergy testing which may yield additional information by showing the intensity of an allergic reaction.

## EXERCISE 8 – HOW BAD IS IT?

### TECHNIQUE: INDIRECT DOWSING

In this instance you are going to use a scale as a means of registering your reaction. Make a scale 20 cm in length. Mark the halfway point so that the scale is divided into two sections. Mark the right-hand section with numbers 1–10 and label it positive. Mark the left-hand section with numbers from minus 10 to minus 1 and label it negative. Put the sampler to be tested at the mid-point. Start dowsing at the minus 10 end of the scale, moving slowly along each calibration. Observe any changes in the reaction of the pendulum. A strong reaction in the lower end of the negative scale indicates that this food does not suit you. A strong action in the positive section gives the all clear.

| NEGATIVE | POSITIVE |
|---|---|

```
                                 0
-10 -9 -8 -7 -6 -5 -4 -3 -2 -1    1  2  3  4  5  6  7  8  9  10
```

Adapted from *Dowsing for Health* by Arthur Bailey

If you are doing this for yourself, you probably do not need to use a witness. If you are doing this for someone else, it is useful to have a lock of their hair. When using a witness in this way I would have one hand over the witness while using the pendulum with the other.

Even if you do not suspect an allergy, you might like to test a variety of food samples to develop your dowsing skills. Of course you may not have any specific allergies at all. However, the ability to tolerate a wide range of foods is not the same as an assessment of their true nutritional value. You can learn a great deal about the many varieties of food available to us as consumers. We are offered frozen food, preserved food, vacuum packed food, dried food, chilled food, organic food, tinned foods, packet foods, artificial foods, natural foods. You might like to gradually dowse them all.

# Mind, body and spirit

*According to Yoga philosophy, there is no lifeless matter, for everything is consciousness itself. Scientists tell us that inside the tiniest particles of atoms is incredible movement. If there is movement, there must be some kind of energy to cause it, and that energy is the basis of all life.*
    Swami Visnuevananda, The Complete Illustrated Book of Yoga

The human being is not merely a collection of physical systems, but a complex interrelationship between matter and energy. The physical body acts as the recorder and magnifier of an extraordinary range of emotional, psychological and spiritual responses. The effects of stress, intense emotion and psychological upsets become lodged in the body though the intermediary of the energy field. The physical body is constantly renewing itself through the regeneration of cells. The energy field acts like a blueprint passing on information about mental and emotional states. The body/mind/spirit unity which we perceive as the human being possesses a natural energy structure which acts as a framework within the individual. Many holistic healing systems are constructed upon the relationship between subtle energy and physical well-being. Physical symptoms indicate an imbalance in the energy field. Acupuncture rebalances these energies directly by activating the nodal points throughout the body. Acupuncture creates change at the physical level by affecting the energy field. Changes within the energy field produce changes

within the physical body. Dowsing can be used to locate energy blockages and imbalances. The healthy body/mind/spirit unity conforms to a naturally occurring configuration. There are fourteen meridian rivers which run in a longitudinal fashion throughout the body. The acupuncture practitioner is able to assess each of these in turn. As the meridians are able to provide information about the internal organs, acupuncture offers a thorough system of diagnosis and intervention. In addition the body/mind/spirit unity has seven centres of energy. If the meridians can be likened to rivers, these centres may be likened to pools. These pools of energy are in constant activity, like whirlpools. They are called wheels. In Sanskrit the word is *chakra*.

The mind/body/spirit unity is in continuous change. The physical body renews itself continuously. The life of the mind, the emotions and the spirit are ever present. The abstract life of thought, feeling and aspiration is translated through the intermediary of the living energy system. An old saying states, 'energy follows thought'. This is an important basic principle in understanding the relationship between mind and body. The energy field itself is highly sensitive to thoughts and intense emotions. It is also responsive to certain remedies which offer more than just physical input.

# Homeopathic medicines – like cures like

Homeopathy is becoming increasingly popular. Unlike allopathic medicine which matches remedy to symptom. Homeopathy matches remedy to the whole person. People respond quite individually to commonly shared infections such as flu. We each have our natural healing mechanism and immune system. Allopathic medicine cannot treat the patient as an individual. Dr Samuel Hahnemann is considered to be the father of modern homeopathy. He experimented with a huge range of remedies and discovered that:

- A medicine which in large doses produces symptoms in small doses will cure.

- Extreme dilution enhances the curative properties and negates the undesirable effects.

- Homeopathic medicines treat the whole person.

There are, however, literally thousands of homeopathic remedies, which makes selecting a remedy a skilled practice. There is no substitute for the attention of a qualified practitioner who will patiently formulate a patient profile in order to select the appropriate remedy. Some practitioners, however, use dowsing as a means of selecting a remedy. In the book *Dowsing for Health*, Arthur Bailey explains how he uses dowsing to help select the appropriate remedy for a patient. We may learn something from his procedures. As a practitioner, Bailey keeps a large number of remedies in stock, stored in boxes. Bailey again stresses the importance of mental discipline in the procedure. 'Dowsing under mental control, you can set up the rules for yourself.' Faced with a large number of remedies, the first task is to make a primary selection. Bailey does this by asking the same question while dowsing over each box. 'Is there a suitable remedy for the patient in this box?' The task is now considerably reduced, a matter of finding the appropriate remedy in the box selected. Bailey approaches this problem by using the tightly packed box as representative of a grid. He dowses the horizontal rows, by asking, 'Is there a remedy for the patient in this row?' This is repeated along the vertical axis by asking, 'Is there a remedy for the patient in this column?' The point of intersection will provide the remedy. At this point Bailey checks the potential remedy, and is careful never to let dowsing override common sense. If he is satisfied, the next task is to assess the potency and daily dose.

## POTENCIES

Homeopathic remedies come in a wide range of potencies. Finding the right potency is as important as finding the right remedy. Bailey assesses the potency by using a scale marked in equal increments. The potencies are listed along the scale. The remedy is placed at one

end of the scale, the patient's witness at the other. He dowses for the maximum reaction.

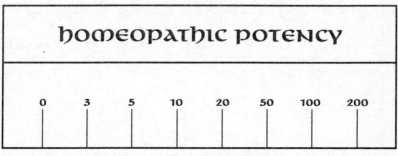

## homeopathic potency

| 0 | 3 | 5 | 10 | 20 | 50 | 100 | 200 |

Adapted from *Dowsing for Health* by Arthur Bailey

## The daily dosage

This is assessed in the same way using a different scale marked from 1 to 10. It is important not to mix scales, even if the calibration is the same. The mental processes being applied to each is different and mixing will certainly cause confusion. Once again, place a sample of the remedy at one end and the patient's witness at the other.

## NUMBER OF DOSES PER DAY

| 0 | 1 | 2 | 3 | 4 | 5 | 6 | 7 | 8 | 9 | 10 |

Adapted from *Dowsing for Health* by Arthur Bailey

## Number of tablets per dose

Use another scale in exactly the same way.

| | | | | | | | | | | |
|---|---|---|---|---|---|---|---|---|---|---|

### NUMBER OF TABLETS PER DOSE

| 0 | 1 | 2 | 3 | 4 | 5 | 6 | 7 | 8 | 9 | 10 |
|---|---|---|---|---|---|---|---|---|---|---|

Adapted from *Dowsing for Health* by Arthur Bailey

## Using Lists

Bailey is a practitioner. He has found this process to be effective and indeed time-saving. What may we as lay persons learn from this process? We do not have a large stock of remedies on the shelf. Bailey himself is aware of this difficulty and has discovered a short cut which anyone can use. It is possible to dowse from a list. Bailey himself says, 'I tried it out and much to my surprise it worked.' I too have dowsed from lists and have found it to be successful as well as fascinating. Like Bailey, I have to admit that 'it is at this point that logical explanations fall away'. We too may dowse from a list. It is a perfectly simple procedure. We can dowse for a remedy by working directly with a list of homeopathic remedies using an amended list from a book on the subject. The complete list of homeopathic remedies is to be found in *Materia Medica*.

### EXERCISE 9 – WHAT DO I NEED?

#### TECHNIQUE: INDIRECT DOWSING

T his process can be applied to any list. Formulate your question clearly. Go through the options repeating the question. If your

list is short, you can keep asking the same question. If your list is long, divide it into manageable sections. For instance you could ask, 'Is there an appropriate remedy for me on this page?' The principle is simple: keep narrowing down the area of search until one option is indicated.

# The healing flowers

Edward Bach was another pioneering medical practitioner and, like Hahnemann, he sought to find a remedy in nature. He too was a most unusual and sensitive man who experienced the full range of symptoms through his own body. His pioneering work and sensitivity created a unique range of subtle medicines.

Edward Bach trained as a doctor but soon became dissatisfied with the forms of treatment available to him. He had a natural interest in herbal remedies and was convinced that nature herself offered undiscovered remedies. In 1930 he began to search out remedies from nature's store cupboard by collecting the dew from plants. Bach was remarkably sensitised to the high and pure energies of the natural world. If he held the petals or blooms, he could feel the effects of the properties within the flower. He found that dew was more potent when collected from plants that grew in sunlight. Collecting dew was not, however, a very practical solution so he began to collect perfect blooms which he placed in water standing in sunlight.

His flower remedies were not intended as cures but to restore the individuals to a state of balance and wholeness. His remedies touched the underlying causes of illness which he identified as 12 mental states. There is no doubt that Edward Bach was ahead of his time, and his sympathies and ideas are much more in keeping with the spirit of our age. He ran a busy practice when he was not actively searching for new remedies, which was a solitary and at times difficult pursuit. He would be greatly surprised but immensely pleased at the way in which his remedies have become a vital aspect of subtle medicine which treats the whole person at all levels.

# The Bach flower remedies

| | |
|---|---|
| **Rock Rose** | *Fear:* terror, panic, fear in extreme |
| **Mimulus** | *Fear:* shyness, timidity, fears with known origin |
| **Cherry Plum** | *Fear:* collapse of mental control, vicious temper, fear of doing harm to others |
| **Aspen** | *Fear:* apprehension, foreboding, vague fears with unknown origin |
| **Red Chestnut** | *Fear:* over-caring and exaggerated fears for others (especially loved ones), anticipates 'the worst' |
| **Cerato** | *Uncertainty:* doubts own judgement, often misguided, seeks guidance from authority-figures |
| **Scleranthus** | *Uncertainty:* indecision, vacillation, fluctuating moods |
| **Gentian** | *Uncertainty:* despondent, easily discouraged, dejected from known cause |
| **Gorse** | *Uncertainty:* extreme hopelessness, despair, pessimism, negativity, fatalism |
| **Hornbeam** | *Uncertainty:* procrastination (but once started task is usually finished) |
| **Wild Oat** | *Uncertainty:* unfulfilled, ambitious but aimless |
| **Clematis** | *Avoiding here and now:* day dreaming, indifference, inattention, escapism |
| **Honeysuckle** | *Avoiding here and now:* nostalgia, reflecting on past pleasures and glories, homesickness |
| **Wild Rose** | *Avoiding here and now:* resignation, apathy, drifting, no ambition |
| **Olive** | *Avoiding here and now:* complete exhaustion, drained of energy, everything is a chore |
| **White Chestnut** | *Avoiding here and now:* preoccupied with persistent unwarranted worries, mental arguments |

| | |
|---|---|
| **Mustard** | *Avoiding here and now:* deep gloom, melancholia, recurrent depression for no known reason |
| **Chestnut Bud** | *Avoiding here and now:* unobservant of life's lessons, repeats some mistakes |
| **Water Violet** | *Loneliness:* clean living, proud, reserved, sedate, sometimes 'superior aloof', capable, independent, reliable |
| **Impatiens** | *Loneliness:* impatient (especially with others), hasty, independent, 'can't wait' quickness |
| **Heather** | *Loneliness:* over-concerned with self, talkative bores, poor listeners, hates to be alone |
| **Agrimony** | *Oversensitivity:* facade of cheerfulness hides inner torture, hides worries from others |
| **Centaury** | *Oversensitivity:* weak-willed, subservient, over anxious to please, 'doormat' tendency, easily exploited |
| **Walnut** | *Oversensitivity:* overwhelmed by powerful influences at present time – normally capable |
| **Holly** | *Oversensitivity:* misanthropy, envy, jealousy, hatred, suspicion |
| **Larch** | *Despondency and despair:* no confidence, expects and fears failure, does not try, unwarranted sense of inferiority |
| **Pine** | *Despondency and despair:* guilt, self reproach, over conscientiousness, feels unworthy, takes blame for others' mistakes |
| **Elm** | *Despondency and despair:* temporarily overwhelmed by responsibility, normally very capable |
| **Sweet Chestnut** | *Despondency and despair:* extreme anguish, desolation, at limit of emotional endurance (non-suicidal) |

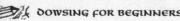 

| Star of Bethlehem | *Despondency and despair:* effect of fright, serious news, great sorrow, trauma etc |
| Willow | *Despondency and despair:* resentment, bitterness, self pity |
| Oak | *Despondency and despair:* at limit of endurance against illness and/or physical adversity |
| Crab Apple | *Despondency and despair:* feels unclean (in mind or body), self-dislike/disgust |
| Chicory | *Overcare:* selfishness, possessiveness, demands respect and obedience |
| Vervain | *Overcare:* over enthusiastic, fanatical, highly strung, incensed by injustices |
| Vine | *Overcare:* domineering, inflexible, ambitious, tyrannical/autocratic |
| Beech | *Overcare:* intolerant, critical, arrogant, judgemental |
| Rock Water | *Overcare:* self-denial, rigid, tight, self-righteous, aims to set an example |

*Avoiding here and now:* Bach's original term was 'Lack of interest in present circumstances'.
*Oversensitivity:* Bach's original term was 'Oversensitivity to influences and ideas'.
*Overcare:* Bach's original term was 'Overcare for others' welfare'.
The *Rescue Remedy* – for emergencies and accidents – is a combination of Cherry Plum, Clematis, Impatiens, Rock Rose and Star of Bethlehem.

Arthur Bailey worked extensively with the Bach remedies. He began to experiment with flowers himself. He too collected flowers and dowsed over the sample asking, 'Do you possess healing properties for humans?' Over an 11-year period, he developed 26 new essences for attitudes of mind. We might wonder how many more remedies are just waiting for someone to ask the right question.

We have looked at how dowsing might help us to find the right remedy for us. In one sense we have not moved all that far from a

conventional outlook. Radionics, however, is a long way from a conventional approach to medicine. There are no remedies, yet it is claimed healing does take place.

# Radionics

*I appreciate that all attempts at a rational explanation seem to fade into non-existence.*

Arthur Bailey, Dowsing for Health

It is clear that dowsing may be used to identify the location of physical illness, but can we do more than just diagnose? Can the pendulum be used to heal, and if so how? Radionic practitioners claim to be able to heal using the pendulum as an integral focus for both diagnosis and remedy. Radionics is based upon the foundations which we have already examined. In *Radionics – Interface with the Ether Field*, David Tansley states that, 'Basic to Radionic theory and practice is the concept that man and all life forms share a common ground, in that they are submerged in the electromagnetic energy field of the earth; and further that each life form has its own electromagnetic field which if sufficiently distorted will ultimately result in disease of the organism. . . . Radionics sees organs, disease and remedies as having their own particular frequencies or vibrations. These factors can be expressed in numerical values.'

Radionics stems from the work of Dr Albert Abrams. He was Professor of Pathology and Director of the Cooper Medical College. He was well qualified as an orthodox doctor but looked beyond orthodoxy. He developed a diaphragm of rubber, 'a stick pad'. This amplified the personal response in the same way that a dowsing instrument works. The finger would stick when a 'yes' response was indicated but would slide smoothly over the pad when a 'no' response was indicated. Abrams elaborated this basic code with a series of rheostats provided with calibrated dials. The end connection was wired into the stick pad. The patient touched a connection at the other end of the series and the dials were adjusted one at a time until the stick, the positive action, was recorded.

Abrams observed that patients suffering the same illness recorded the same six digit code. This enabled him to create an extensive code book in which diseases were recorded as a series of numbers. Abrams' invention of the Black Box seemed to work as an additional diagnostic tool. It was, in effect, making the subconscious of the patient visible, rendering it in a numerical form. Nor can we deny the role of Abrams' own subconscious in the formulation of the code book. However, that is no bad thing, as it is clear that the subconscious possesses an intrinsic wisdom searching for visible expression. Abrams moved on from diagnosing from the actual patient, to diagnosing from a witness, using a sample, most often a lock of hair. As a doctor, Abrams was just as concerned with remedy as diagnosis. If a disease could be codified, it occurred to him that its remedy might be codified. He worked in exactly the same way, testing patients with known diseases and re-tuning the dials one at a time until each dial recorded a positive response. He produced another set of rates.

It has to be said that the explanations of the Black Box made no rational sense whatsoever. Abrams had created a scientific-looking machine and he needed to justify it, in at least pseudo-scientific terms, in an age which demanded a scientific rationale. He was ridiculed and at one point was taken to court. However, he still claimed success for his Black Box. His ideas were picked up by others, most notably George and Marjorie de la Warre. They were interested enough to continue research and development, and Abrams' Black Box was followed by the de La Warre Black Box, a more sophisticated version of the original. They set up a laboratory and experimented at the very forefront of the etheric interface. Unfortunately no one since has been able to follow in their footsteps. The laboratory even developed a Radio-Vision instrument. Photographs were obtained by placing a blood sample in the machine. The rates were set up on the dial. They claimed to have produced some 12,000 radionic photographs, including images obtained from homeopathic remedies. One spectacular image does look very much like a foetus. It reportedly came from a blood spot taken from a woman who was three months pregnant. However, the photographic plates only developed in the presence of certain

people, most notably their collaborator Ruth Drown, who had high hopes for their research, stated (*Radionics – Interface with the Ether Field*, by David Tansley): 'New research is carrying this work to a higher plane of achievement, with no end in sight to what may be recorded by these methods. New designs in the instruments, moving constantly towards even simpler arrangements are revealing ways to tap into cosmic laws and secrets never hitherto accessible to man. Special sensitised materials and devices open incredible new vistas for the human race.' These high aspirations never materialised. Quite simply, no one other than Ruth Drown herself was able to sensitise the plates. This fact does not invalidate her work, but rather highlights one of the major difficulties of all original work in this area. The instrument ultimately is the operator; there is no such thing as the ultimate instrument. Edward Bach was another highly sensitive person. He only had to hold a flower to feel its potency. He experienced all the symptoms in his own body. How many people could replicate this for themselves?

The Black Box worked not by virtue of its essential parts, as we shall see. Nevertheless, it permitted a transaction to take place at some level below the threshold of consciousness. The more we try to explain how this transaction might be effected, the more we begin to flounder. We truly cannot provide a full account of this interaction, yet despite this it does seem to work. The de la Warres were taken to court by a woman who claimed she had suffered mental illness from trying to make the box work, but the de la Warres won their case. The judge said that though he did not understand how the box worked, evidence had been produced to support its effectiveness.

Arthur Bailey was intrigued by the Black Box and built one of his own. It worked for him. Next he built a modified version, a grey box. It also worked. However, as he freely admitted, 'It worked very well but there is just one problem: there is nothing inside it.' Having taken out all the possible working parts, the next step is to remove all the moving parts and pare the principle down to its very essentials.

Take a long strip of paper. Write down the numbers 0–9. If available, have the witness in one hand and commence dowsing. Dowse each number in turn while thinking 'I am dowsing to broadcast a

treatment rate.' Some numbers will react positively, others will not react at all.

The ultimate solution is to throw away the code itself. Take a lock of hair or just think about the person and begin to broadcast healing.

I have been doing just this with some rather peculiar results. I do not claim to have worked any miracles. The pendulum reacts quite differently when I use it this way. I find that if I seek healing for someone who has no need of it, the pendulum hardly moves at all. But if someone is really in need of healing the pendulum moves with great force and intensity. It seems for me, then, that activity of the pendulum mirrors the degree of need in the patient.

You can try this for yourself. You certainly can do no harm and you might do some good.

## Choosing

There are times when it is appropriate to work for others; there are also times when it is appropriate to employ dowsing for yourself too.

Everyday life is full of decisions. Most decisions are simple and momentary, others are more difficult. When making a decision we are in effect attempting to evaluate the long-term consequences of a given action. Of course we cannot know the long-term consequences of significant decisions, like changing job, so we try to make as full an assessment as possible by taking all factors into account. Sometimes we find it hard even to know our own minds. There can be a conflict of interest between what we feel we should want, and what we really want for ourselves. Dowsing is a good way of getting in touch with our true feelings, especially if we are aware of a conflict. For instance personal weight can become a painful issue. Women especially are under pressure to conform to a certain size and weight. This external pressure slowly becomes internalised and can cause a lot of unhappiness. Dowsing can be very helpful in finding out what you really feel, not what you think.

## EXERCISE – WHAT DO I REALLY WANT?

### TECHNIQUE: INDIRECT DOWSING

**Changing weight**

- Do I feel happy about myself as I am?

- Do I really want to change myself through weight loss/gain?

- Is the ideal weight for me . . . ?

You can of course add questions of your own which reflect your own circumstances and feelings. Don't be surprised when the pendulum doesn't uphold your conscious desires. They may not be what you really want.

You have covered a lot of ground in a short time, and perhaps now would be a good time to check back over the first chapters to see how much you have remembered.

### PRACTICE QUESTIONS FOR CHAPTERS 1–3

- What is meant by a 'life-field' and how can they be 'recorded'?

- Give some examples of pendulums.

- How many techniques for dowsing can you describe?

- What is the Mager Rosette and how is it used?

- How can you find your own energy field?

- How can you use dowsing to find out if certain foods are good for you?

- How can dowsing help you to decide on the right remedy for you in times of ill health?

# 4 the wheels of life

*The whole process is, as you can see one of development, use and transference, as is the case in all evolutionary development.*

Alice Bailey, Ponder on This

The word *chakra* simply means wheel. Chakras are also described as lotuses, *padmas*. This symbolic description tells us a great deal. A lotus is a beautiful flower, rather like a water lily. It is rooted in the mud but eventually flowers on the surface of the water. We can deepen our understanding of this symbolism through the following visualisation.

## EXERCISE 1 – The LOTUS

Imagine that you are seated by a pool. The surface of the water is dotted with lotus plants. Some of these are already coming into bloom. As you look over the water, you can see that some plants are just budding. Other flowers are just opening. In the centre of the pool, one flower has reached its full beauty. Its many petals are open. You glance at the partially opened blooms, knowing that when all the lotuses are fully opened, the pool will be a truly beautiful sight.

It is usual to speak of seven chakras. However, strictly speaking there are only six. The seventh is quite unlike the others. Having said that, it is usual to describe the system as being sevenfold, and we will follow this schema. The vitality and balance of this system underpins our total well-being at all levels – physical, emotional, mental, and spiritual. The chakras are themselves multi-levelled and

relate to the total person. At the physical level, they act as reservoirs of energy for various physical systems. A chakra corresponds to each of the systems of excretion, reproduction, digestion, circulation, respiration, and cognition. The seventh chakra is not limited to a physical system.

The chakras are to be found strung upon the length of the spine starting at the base. Each chakra is therefore related to the spinal

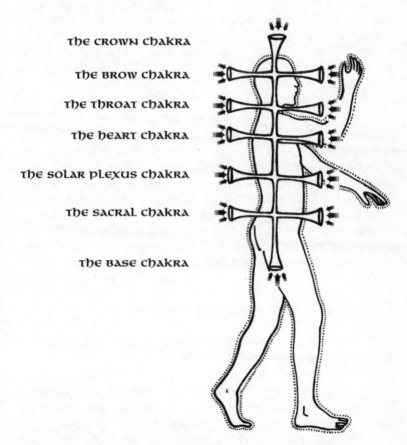

the CROWN chakra

the BROW chakra

the THROAT chakra

the HEART chakra

the SOLAR PLEXUS chakra

the SACRAL chakra

the BASE chakra

Adapted from *Hands of Light* by Barbara Brennan (Bantam Books, 1988), showing front and back views.

nerves which regulate the various systems. If the reservoir is empty, the corresponding organs which are fed by the chakra will be under-vitalised and will eventually show damage, producing imbalance in the related physical systems, which we recognise as ill health. In other words, when the base chakra is malfunctioning we can expect problems to manifest through the system of excretion. If the sacral chakra is malfunctioning we can expect difficulties in the reproductive system. If the solar plexus is unbalanced we can expect problems in the system of digestion. On one occasion I did a chakra profile for an elderly gentleman. The reading from his solar plexus chakra was unusually large. I asked him about his health. He was a diabetic. Particular physical problems are related to a specific chakra. This reciprocal relationship provides the opportunity for diagnosis and intervention. If the energy level of the chakra is changed, it will create a change in the vitality of the organs to which it is related.

However, the chakras are multi-levelled and function at emotional, mental and spiritual levels too. In many cases the chakra is dormant at the higher levels. Strictly speaking each chakra functions at seven levels. This is a measure of our potential growth. We are in truth a sevenfold being. Therefore each chakra also corresponds to the emotional and mental states related to the physical system. For instance, physically the sacral chakra corresponds to the reproductive system, emotionally to our interpersonal relationships and mentally to our outlook on sexuality, intimacy and nurturing.

# Wheels and rivers

The physical body is interpenetrated by meridians which carry vitality throughout the body. These rivers of energy are punctuated by nodes, the acupuncture points. It is possible to locate these points through dowsing if you are familiar with subtle anatomy. However, these points are small and easy to miss. It is relatively easy to dowse the chakras, which create large energy fields. Previously you worked with the left/right polarity of the body; you now need to dowse along the central axis of the body. Use the following locations for them.

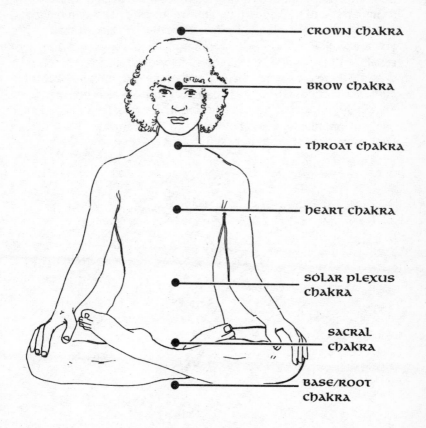

CROWN chakra

BROW chakra

THROAT chakra

heart chakra

solar plexus chakra

sacral chakra

BASE/ROOT chakra

## EXERCISE 2

### TECHNIQUE: DIRECT DOWSING

You will need a friend to act as a volunteer for you. Ask your friend to lay out flat, making sure they are comfortable. Using the diagram, suspend your pendulum in the approximate location, as usual you will need to experiment to find the optimum distance from the body and this will vary from person to person. It is sometimes hard to differentiate the two lowest chakras from each other, but the solar plexus chakra is usually very easy to find. When you are working directly with another person, always be especially sensitive. It is possible to destabilise someone through their energy system. Therefore do not act on the chakras with anything but the highest intentions. Keep your sessions short. Some people are extremely sensitive. If you should feel in any way light-headed after chakra work then rest and have a warm drink and call a halt to chakra work for at least the rest of the day.

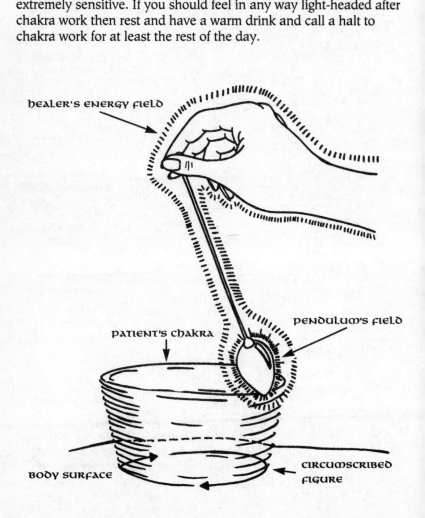

HEALER'S ENERGY FIELD

PENDULUM'S FIELD

PATIENT'S CHAKRA

CIRCUMSCRIBED FIGURE

BODY SURFACE

Barbara Brennan is a chakra therapist. She writes in *Hands of Light*: 'As the therapist becomes more proficient in the use of the pendulum, they will begin to observe more qualities in their measurements, the rate of swing (how fast the pendulum moves) indicates the amount of energy being metabolised through the chakra. With practice, the therapist can also pick up "qualities" such as tension, exuberance, heaviness, sadness, grief, peacefulness and clarity.'

Of course locating the chakras through dowsing is by itself rather meaningless: you need to be able to interpret the responses. In order to be able to do this more fully we need to expand the functions of each chakra. When you dowse you are liable to encounter:

- A clockwise gyration.

- An anticlockwise gyration.

- A horizontal oscillation.

- A vertical oscillation.

- No movement at all.

Other variations are possible, but these are the most common.

| | |
|---|---|
| **Clockwise** | open, feelings governed by the chakras are integrated and balanced, physical system should be functioning. |
| **Anticlockwise** | closed, feelings governed by the chakra are not assimilated, physical systems not fully functional. |
| **Horizontal oscillation** | holding energy, a strong block, noticeable resistance to the feelings associated with the chakra, physical symptoms are likely to be due to repressed emotions. |
| **Vertical oscillation** | energies being focused from the personal towards the spiritual, some physical disturbance likely. |
| **Standstill** | no energy being circulated, will lead to physical symptoms. |

We need to apply these responses to each chakra. A clockwise response indicates that the energies of the chakra are being used, the corresponding physical system should be healthy, the emotions corresponding to the chakra will be apparent in the attitude to life. A clockwise reaction indicates that the powers of the chakra are not being used. I regard this as a state of dormancy since it does not always show the negative results of a blocked chakra.

A strong horizontal swing indicates the presence of a block. I have found that this is invariably linked with physical consequences. I dowsed the chakras of a young woman whose sacral chakra showed a block. She told me she had been actively trying to conceive and had been unsuccessful. A client came to me in my capacity as a hypnotherapist complaining of impotence. A therapy session revealed no psychological reasons, but a dowsing session showed an energy imbalance in the sacral chakra. I suggested acupuncture as a way of redressing the imbalance. He rang me up a few weeks later to say that the treatment had been successful. I encountered a total standstill in a sacral chakra of a friend while she was in the grip of cystitis. I recently encountered an unusual case: all chakras registered blocked. This woman had experienced a nervous breakdown and was undergoing regular therapy. I asked her how she felt and she said 'terrible'.

We may look at the physical, emotional and mental qualities connected with each chakra to provide reference points for practical dowsing.

## The Base Chakra

Physical system – excretion.
Body parts – large intestine, legs and feet.
Psychological keyword – belonging.
Open chakra – sense of being grounded, survival instinct, ability to let go of the past and emotions, the ability to stand on your own two feet.
Closed chakra – poorly developed sense of reality.

Blocked chakra – insecurity, depression, inability to release the past.
Malfunction – tendency to haemorrhoids, constipation, sciatica, prostate problems in men.

## tbe sacral cbakra

Physical system – reproduction.
Body parts – womb, kidney, bladder.
Psychological keyword – relating.
Open chakra – ability to relate to others, ability to share, self confidence.
Closed chakra – selfish, self centred, unfeeling.
Blocked chakra – inability to sustain relationships.
Malfunction – tendency to menstrual problems, impotence, frigidity, kidney or bladder problems.

## tbe solar plexus cbakra

Physical system – digestion.
Body parts – stomach.
Psychological keyword – direction.
Open chakra – sense of direction in life, willingness to take personal responsibility for actions, a controlled will, self determination.
Closed chakra – sense of powerlessness, lack of self esteem, lack of direction in life.
Blocked chakra – weak, easily swayed by others, no sense of self.
Malfunction – tendency to ulcers, eating disorders.

## tbe beart cbakra

Physical system – circulation.
Body parts – heart, lungs.
Psychological keyword – compassion.
Open chakra – transpersonal love, compassion, openness, acceptance.

Closed chakra – lack of emotional depth.
Blocked chakra – inability to empathise.
Malfunction – tendency to hypertension, angina.

## THE THROAT CHAKRA

Physical system – respiration.
Body parts – lungs, throat.
Psychological keyword – creativity.
Open chakra – good powers of communication, self expression, creativity.
Closed chakra – inability to express inner self, sense of frustration.
Blocked chakra – cannot express emotions or ideas verbally.
Malfunction – tendency to sore throats, losing the voice unexpectedly.

## THE BROW CHAKRA

Physical system – mentation.
Body parts – the brain and eyes.
Psychological keyword – intuition.
Open chakra – imaginative, creative, visual, has lucid dreams, intuitive.
Closed chakra – fantasies without meaning, dependence on rationality.
Blocked chakra – lack of imagination, prosaic outlook.
Malfunction – tendency to headaches, fuzzy thinking, mental confusion.

## THE CROWN CHAKRA

Physical system – not relevant.
Body parts – not relevant.
Psychological keyword – awakening.

Open chakra – aware of human potential growth, consciously on the path of self realisation.
Closed chakra – unaware of potential, dependence on a physical explanation of reality.
Blocked chakra – alienation, isolation, a closed mind.

## EXERCISE 3 – THE CHAKRA PROFILE

Describe a person whose chakra profile reads as follows:

7. **Crown chakra** horizontal oscillation.
6. **Brow chakra** – anticlockwise gyration.
5. **Throat chakra** – clockwise gyration.
4. **Heart chakra** – anticlockwise gyration.
3. **Solar plexus chakra** – clockwise gyration.
2. **Sacral chakra** – clockwise gyration.
1. **Base chakra** – clockwise gyration.

The energy system is in a constant state of movement. Dowsing a given chakra on one occasion is like taking a snapshot. Chakras respond on a daily basis to our emotions, not thoughts. Over a longer period, they reflect our general attitudes and outlook on life. A person with a materialistic philosophy will be strongly open at the base and solar plexus chakras but will have poorly developed heart and head chakras. A spiritually inclined person will function consciously through the higher centres as well as the lower ones. The seven chakras taken together represent a blueprint of being. We become truly ourselves as we integrate each new level. Dowsing can show us how we are integrating this process. Growth is all about change. Growth cannot take place without change. As we change, the chakras also change.

## EXERCISE 4 – OBSERVING CHANGE

### TECHNIQUE – DIRECT DOWSING

If your friend is willing, arrange to monitor the chakras for a given period – perhaps a month. Beware of strong emotions, both

positive and negative, transpersonal experiences and spiritual practices. Are you able to correlate changes in a chakra with life events?

We might usefully apply what we have learned from radionics. It is possible, as we know, to arrive at a numerical value for a given response. We can construct a code which will serve as a measured reference for chakra work. This might be useful in diagnosing from a witness, and you will need to have a clear understanding of the location and function of the chakras for this operation to be successful. So you may need to undertake some background reading before you try this exercise.

| cLosed | opeN |
|---|---|

|  | 0 |  |
|---|---|---|
| -10 -9 -8 -7 -6 -5 -4 -3 -2 -1 | | 1 2 3 4 5 6 7 8 9 10 |

Adapted from *Dowsing for Health* by Arthur Bailey

Construct a table as shown in the diagram and focus your mind on the chakras one at a time.

- 'Is this chakra open?' . . .
- 'I am searching for a numerical value to show me the degree of openness of this chakra.'

or

- 'Is this chakra closed?' . . .
- 'I am searching for a numerical value to show me the degree of closure of this chakra.'

Dowse over each number in turn until you get an affirmation through the pendulum. This more detailed reference has a value. All growth work, whether as therapy or spiritual discipline, has a

profound effect on the chakras system. Inevitably inner work precipitates crises in the energy blueprint. A block is released, energy shifts, a transformation is effected. A feedback process is always valuable. It is a learning process.

## EXERCISE 5 – PERSONAL GROWTH

### TECHNIQUE – INDIRECT DOWSING

Monitor your own chakras over a given period using this system. It is not possible to physically dowse all of your own chakras, but you can achieve the same thing using this system to correlate life changes to any sudden observed swings in the activity of a chakra. As Barbara Brennan reminds us, 'the process of changing one's belief system redirects chakra movement'. It is possible that learning to dowse might trigger such a process for you.

When you are a confident dowser and have had some experience of working directly with the chakras, it is possible to dowse the higher aspects of the chakras, if you have awakened them within yourself first. You will find that as you move up into the higher levels, the response of the pendulum becomes much fainter. However, don't be put off by the enormity of this challenge. You may learn a great deal.

### PRACTICE QUESTIONS FOR CHAPTER 4

- What does the word *chakra* mean?
- How many chakras are there? Can you name them?
- What are 'meridians'?
- What are the most common responses when dowsing over the chakras?

# 5 THE EARTH MYSTERIES

*The noblest of all Earth's memories is the august ritual of the ancient mysteries.*

A.E. (George William Russell), The Candle of Vision

We live upon the surface of the earth and forget that beneath our feet and our homes lies a subterranean world of different mineral deposits, rock strata and underground streams. It is easy to forget that this underground world may interact with our own in a variety of ways. Is it possible that we can learn something about the world beneath our feet, as both geology and history, from the practice of dowsing? Finding out about the past is a matter for historians and archaeologists. Nevertheless the past fascinates us all, for we are all connected to it. The British Isles are steeped in accessible history. We have an extraordinary number of ancient sites, stone circles, barrows, standing stones, holy wells and sacred springs. The past is all around us. Dowsing shares a common folklore with the ancient earth traditions such as Feng Shui. These earth-centred philosophies have always maintained that living energies permeate the land. The sophisticated scientific equipment of today means that it is at least possible to test sites for various recognised energies such as magnetism and electrical discharge.

## THE SACRED STONES

The British Isles are dotted with stone circles and single megaliths, and we are fascinated. These great stones belong to our ancestral

past. Yet we have become so distanced from an earth-centred wisdom that, while we are awed at the achievement, we are also a little mystified at their purpose. Twentieth century astro-archaeology has enabled us to take a new perspective on the megalithic builders. We take our time from the calendar. These people had to build a calendar for themselves. There is little doubt that many stone circles were used to make the seasonal turning points, the twin solstices. In this way the pattern of the year could be followed. In truth, we still have much to learn about the wisdom of our forefathers who planned and constructed these sites with such care. We have some idea of how the stones were constructively used. We are able to say less about the actual reason for specific locations, which might have been social, practical, esoteric, or even geological. Might there be some association between underground features, the location of sacred sites and the characteristic features of the ancient megaliths themselves?

Reginald Allender Smith was a distinguished archaeologist and amateur dowser. He was also the Keeper of the British and Roman Antiquities Department of the British Museum, and Director of the Society of Antiquaries. In 1939 he addressed the British Society of Dowsers and expressed the belief that blind springs were to be found underneath stone circles, which he describes as 'prehistoric temples'. A blind spring is created when water rises naturally but fails to break surface and radiates horizontally in one or more underground streams. Guy Underwood also believed in the importance of underground water. However, he was at pains to point out that subterranean water is rarely found in free-flowing streams. It is found 'usually at considerable depth and pressure, forcing itself through the beds of gravel or sand, or narrow fissures in the rock trying to find an outlet where its pressure can be relieved.' After many years of dowsing, Underwood coined the term 'geodetic lines', which covered several different kinds of discernible influence. He dowsed at many ancient and historical sites, including Stonehenge, the White Horse, the Cerne Abbas Giant, the cathedrals at Winchester, Salisbury, Chichester and even at Westminster Abbey. His findings were published posthumously in *The Patterns of the Past*.

Bill Lewis, a contemporary and much respected dowser, upholds much the same view. He goes on to say that a standing stone is placed at a crossing point of two or more streams. Lewis is trained as an electrical engineer. He maintains that the movement of water creates a small static electrical field, and believes that the standing stone placed above on the surface amplifies this field further. No worldwide study has been made to investigate the relationship between sacred sites and the surrounding geological features. The ceremonial site, the *Althing* in Iceland, is on the mid Atlantic rift. The Serpent mound in Ohio is situated in an area where there is a collection of faults. In the 1960s John Michell suspected that standing stones in Britain occurred near fault lines. The geologist Paul McCartney found that stone circles were situated within a mile of a surface fault. The bigger henges did not conform to this pattern however. The Belgian Pierre Meraux also located this relationship at Carnac which is hemmed in by faulting. Major Scott Elliot, President of the Scottish Board of Antiquaries believed that stone circles were consciously built over underground geological faults.

Fault zones produce high mineralisation. These zones are simply more active with above average fissuring. German researchers have referred to these as geopathic stress zones. In the 1970s Jakob Stangle investigated the relationship between water-bearing fissures and gamma radiation. He measured unusually high emanations with the aid of a scintillation counter. Dowsers have long held the view that certain underground formations, water-filled fissures, certain mineral veins and geological fractures have an impact on the immediate environment. Such effects may even be potentially harmful to human health. Radon-bearing granite, for example, is now recognised as being a health hazard. It was once thought that radon was confined to the granite-bearing rocks of the south-west, but in 1990 the environmental protection agency conducted a survey and found unexpectedly high levels in Somerset, Derbyshire, Yorkshire, Northamptonshire as well as Cornwall and Devon. It seems that the presence of radon is not exclusive to uranium-bearing rocks but to the presence of water-bearing fissures and fractures. This supports the view that underground streams, often

referred to as black streams, produce effects which are in the long run damaging to human health.

During the 1930s, Pierre Cody, a French engineer, investigated a local phenomenon in Le Havre. He was interested in a number of houses where people consistently developed cancer. He wanted to test the ionisation of the air. He used a gold leaf electroscope which consisted of a pair of gold leaves suspended from an electrical conductor attached to the outside of an insulating box. The operator charged the gold leaves, causing them to repel. Under normal conditions the leaves collapse very slowly, but in ionised air they collapse more quickly. The greater the ionisation, the faster the collapse. Cody discovered that houses in his study were ionised to an unusual degree. He also found that ionisation increased with temperature, showing a daily and also seasonal variation, rising to a maximum in autumn. Cody continued with other tests and finally concluded that the radiation on these sites was in fact radon.

Is it possible that the same effects that are inherently inimical for human habitation provide conditions and circumstances which suit the sacred enclosure as a place set apart? Paul Devereux has been instrumental in setting up the Dragon Project. This is a long-running investigative and assessment programme. Many cold hours have been spent out in the open with monitoring devices. The results have been interesting and point to possible future approaches.

In the 1980s the Dragon Project measured radioactivity at various sites. At the Welsh site of Moel ty Uchaf higher readings were obtained in the north-west quadrant of the circle. In 1983, at a site known as Long Meg, in Cumbria, small zones on three stones emitted constant streams of radiation. The Scottish site, Easter Aquorthies was monitored for 12 hours over a major moonset standstill period in 1978. One huge flare was measured within the circle while the background radiation remained the same. At the moment of moonset the positions were reversed for a short time. Devereux noticed that in areas of high natural radiation such as the south-west, the dolmen, the enclosed granite chamber was more commonly found. This led him to record the radiation within such structures: 'They were environments of enhanced natural radiation,

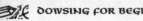 

typically two or three times the local, already high, background radiation.'

Devereux also reported that a most curious phenomenon had been observed in relation to these enclosed granite chambers: a soft, scintillating white light moving across the surface, its nature unknown. Of course granite is well known for its piezo-electrical qualities. The project has also investigated magnetism at various sites. In the mid 1970s magnetic anomalies were revealed at the 4 metre high, Llangynidr Stone near Crickhowell, Wales. These findings corresponded to those discovered by a dowser. In 1983, at the Rollright stones, one stone in the western sector fluctuated quite dramatically for a few hours. Another researcher, Charles Broker, also located magnetically pulsing stones in the same circle. At another Welsh site, Carn Ingli, Hill of the Angels, the hill has a reputation for localised phenomena. Devereux reported magnetic anomalies here. The rocks here have a very high iron content and record an imprint of the magnetic field belonging to the very distant past. Using a liquid-filled compass, Charles Devereux discovered magnetic stones at Castlerigg and at Gors Fawr. Magnetic stones have also been found in Scotland and in the United States. At Mount Tamalpauis, outside San Francisco, four powerspots were identified by a native American elder.

The dowser Bill Lewis shows a remarkable sensitivity to the force channelled by the stones. This is not uncommon among dowsers. We are reminded of the sensitivity of Bach. Lewis also said that the force spiralled up the stone: 'If I feel it building up in my body, I back away very quickly.' In a controlled experiment he was asked to mark where he felt the stone's field pass through his hands. Professor John Taylor then tested the stone with a gaussmeter at ten centimetre intervals. Some of the places indicated by Lewis recorded a strength double that recorded on parts not especially indicated by him.

Lewis' colleague John Williams is also sensitised to these energies. He experiences anything from a mild tingle to a sharp and painful jolt. In the history of dowsing, such extreme reactions are not unfamiliar. Barthélemy Bléton, who later went on to become famous

for his dowsing skills, experienced a similar reaction as a child. At about the age of seven he had taken dinner out to a group of workmen. He sat down on the stone when he was overcome with giddiness and a fainting sensation. Whenever the young Barthélemy moved away from the stone he recovered his composure, but the sensations returned if he sat on the stone again. The vast majority of people are quite insensitive to such forces. It has already been suggested that the stones themselves amplify whatever natural energies are present at the site. Tom Graves, a contemporary authority on dowsing, records in *The Dowser's Workbook* an incident when a friend attempted to amplify the already amplified forces. Tom Graves refers to him simply as 'Peter', probably to spare his blushes. Peter had constructed an ankh. It was nearly two feet high and made from a substantial wire. He wanted to see if it could pick up energy from the circle: 'He climbed onto the roof of a car at the Stonehenge car park and, holding the ankh by the loop at the top and pointing the open end away from him, he moved the ankh like a scanning radar aerial. The moment this aerial came into line with the stones, he felt an enormous surge of power that seemed to burn his arm, and he lost consciousness for a moment. When he recovered he found that he had been, as another friend put it – "thrown bodily off the car" and his arm seemed to be paralysed. It took six months before he was able to use the arm fully again.'

The Dragon Project has also undertaken some experiments in ultrasound. In the 1970s, the early results were interesting. Ultrasound signals were obtained at the Rollright Stones around sunrise. More sophisticated apparatus did not come until 1987, when a clear ultrasound signal was picked up at sunrise from the tallest stone in the circle. Devereux says: 'We are not sure if the sandstone pillar was truly emitting ultrasound, or whether it was acting as a dielectric waveguide for cosmic or artificial electromagnetic waves that triggered the ultrasound receiver.'

What can we make of all this? Clearly here is an area awaiting further research. However, you may conduct some small-scale research of your own. The British Isles is literally dotted with ancient stones. There cannot be many counties that have no access to such

historical sites whether great or small. From the preceding, we can see that even a single stone might provide several different dowsing opportunities. Always treat ancient sites with a degree of respect.

One summer I visited a small stone circle in Kent with a group of friends. We tramped along a path running at the side of a field, climbed a stile and began to make our final approach to the site. We walked along a broad pathway. I had not visited the site before, so I had no idea how close we actually were. I held my L Rods as I walked along. Suddenly both rods swung strongly to the right. I walked on and both my rods turned even more sharply. I looked up, and found that we had arrived: there on my right I could see the stones. The site was actually raised above us at that point. The path we had followed cut right round the base of the hillside. As a group we spent most of the afternoon in the circle. We all had a go at dowsing. I had experienced that first strong pull on approaching the circle. Several people discovered that the stones reacted in a positive/negative way around the circle. Like many existing stone circles, this site is not a great tourist attraction and we had the whole site to ourselves all afternoon.

## EXERCISE 1 – THE SACRED SITE

### TECHNIQUE: DIRECT DOWSING

If you have the opportunity to dowse at a site, take a variety of dowsing tools. A tape measure and compass might also be useful. If you are going to dowse a large object such as a standing stone, dowsing rods are the first choice. Approach the stone from all directions.

- Can you detect an energy field around the stone?

- Is this the same for all the stones on site?

- Do you find any polarised relationships between any stones?

- Is the energy field constant at all times of day and at all seasons of the year?

- Are you able to detect anything using only the palms of your hands?

---

## EXERCISE 2 – BLIND SPRINGS

### TECHNIQUE: DIRECT DOWSING

Several researchers believe that underground water is implicated at megalithic sites, so be prepared to dowse for water at various places on the site. If possible, dowse for water around the base of the stone to see if it is placed over a stream. You should also try the centre of the site, if the stones have been arranged in a circle. Be prepared to try rods of different kinds here. The bobber might be useful when dealing with large energy fields. This might also be a good opportunity to try out the geologist's dowsing wand. There are many mysteries connected with ancient sites. These great stones were placed with intent. Always be prepared for the unexpected: this is the joy of dowsing.

### TECHNIQUE: INDIRECT DOWSING

You might like to try your hand at indirect dowsing. There is plenty of opportunity to apply it in relation to historical subjects. Bill Lewis and John Williams together use dowsing as a means of accessing information. The following session shows how a simple question and answer technique can be expanded to give substantially more information.

**Q.** What year was the stone taken from the river?
**A.** 5636 BC

**Q.** What month of the year?
**A.** August

**Q.** How many tons is the stone?
**A.** Twelve

**Q.** How many people were used to transport it?
**A.** 31

**Q.** What ages were the oldest men?
**A.** 33

**Q.** What ages were the youngest men?
**A.** 34

**Q.** What ages were the oldest women?
**A.** 33

**Q.** What ages were the youngest women?
**A.** 24

**Q.** How many days did it take to transport the stone?
**A.** 6

**Q.** How many days did it take to erect the stone?
**A.** 2

**Q.** How far into the ground does the stone extend?
**A.** 6

**Q.** Are there cremation ashes buried underneath it?
**A.** No

**Q.** Was the stone used daily by the tribe?
**A.** No

**Q.** Was the stone used on tribal ceremonial occasions?
**A.** Yes

**Q.** How many times a year did the tribal ceremonies take place?
**A.** 8

**Q.** Did they take place on the same days in every year?
**A.** No

**Q.** Did the phases of the moon influence which day the ceremonies were held?
**A.** Yes

## EXERCISE 3 – ARMCHAIR DOWSING

### TECHNIQUE: INDIRECT DOWSING

You might like to try your hand dowsing at the most ancient site of all, Stonehenge. You can try this experiment from the comfort of your own armchair. You might like to try the following questions:

- When do you think the ditch surrounding the monument was begun?

- How many cubic metres of chalk do you think were quarried to make up the inner bank?

- How many man hours were required to dig it out?

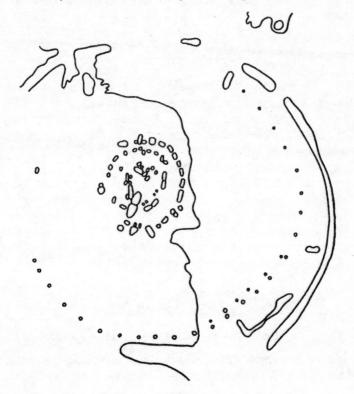

- Was Stonehenge used as an observatory?
- Was Stonehenge used to predict eclipses?

## EXERCISE 4 – TELL ME MORE

### TECHNIQUE: INDIRECT DOWSING

We all have an interest in the past. There is no reason why we should not ally this interest to dowsing. Using your favourite historical period, compile a list of questions to which you would genuinely like to have an answer. Use your dowsing ability to generate responses. At the end of the session honestly assess your results. Are they within the parameters of common sense, or are they wildly inaccurate? Compare your answers with historical sources if possible.

## When did it happen?

History is commonly thought to be about dates – which of course it is not. However, dating is both interesting and important to historical study. Accepted dates are revised more than once by historians as new techniques become available. Dowsers too have been interested in dating procedures. Dr JH Fiddler used a thirty inch pendulum with a pack of cards 1, 2, 4, 8, 16 etc., using fourteen cards in all. He suspended the pendulum over the spot on the map or the subject he was trying to date. He placed his left forefinger over each card in turn, putting the 'yes' cards in a pile. Finally he totalled the digits. Major Scott Elliot counted aloud in thousands, then hundreds and then tens and let the pendulum show him when to stop.

## EXERCISE 5 – HOW OLD IS IT?

### TECHNIQUE: INDIRECT DOWSING

Make a selection of historical pictures; postcards from museums are ideal. Attempt to date them using dowsing. Try both of the

methods suggested. Which do you prefer? Why not make up your own method? Dowsing always works best when you have designed your own system.

So far we have discussed a possible relationship between ancient stone monuments and geophysical characteristics. Could it be that the strange phenomena witnessed and recorded at these sites are the very effects which have given rise to the notion of black streams, places possessed by an unhealthy geopathic energy?

## Black streams

It has long been held that certain locations are not beneficial for human habitation. According to Ralph Whitlock, black streams have a wide variety of negative effects. He suggests that the following results arise from a proximity to a so-called 'black stream'. People who sleep in such a spot are more liable to insomnia, rheumatism and arthritis, and are more likely to contract cancer. Farm animals housed in such buildings also display symptoms of ill health. Domestic and laboratory animals confined to pens on such sites will become aggressive. Wild animals will avoid such zones. Preserved food will keep badly, and wine and cider do not store well. Some species of tree will evidence disease: apples develop canker, although oak, willow, poplar and elm thrive at such spots. What is it about an underground stream that might cause an invisible but potent negative reaction? Might it be the friction produced by the flow of water? French dowsers discovered concentrations of ions above the water. However, when recognised, such spots can be neutralised.

Arthur Bailey recorded, in *Dowsing and Church Archaeology*, his first experience at neutralising such a black stream. 'I was asked if I could check on an arts centre not far away on the Yorkshire Dales. The two ladies who ran the place lived on the premises, which used to be a small country church. I dowsed around the building with angle rods and the Mager Rosette. I found that I experienced two strong reactions: one stream just missed the building and the other cut right under it just by the entrance porch. Never having tried my hand at such a thing before, I dowsed for what length of iron I

needed for each stream, and for the point to hammer the iron into the ground.' Bailey began hammering the angle iron into the ground. 'There was an immediate release of energies. The downstream side of the rod dowsed quite clearly as black on the rosette, but the upstream side felt strange. The experience I had was of being surrounded by swirling hostile energies.

This I had not expected. I was rather startled and worried. Upstream from the rod the stream flowed under the road which led up into the Dales. I was concerned that someone sensitive could react to the effect when driving a car, and perhaps have an accident. I therefore went upstream from the road, into the car park, and put down an extra rod for each of the streams here. That seemed to do the trick and the road felt perfectly OK.'

It is curious that such black streams are invariably defused by being staked in the appropriate place with an iron rod. The vampire imagery is unmistakable, indeed the black stream functions much as the traditional vampire is supposed to do, sucking the vitality and energy of those sharing the same spot. We might also recall the tale of St George and the dragon. The earth energy has long been called the dragon current and St George has a mythical connection with high places.

Dowsing opens up new avenues and possibilities for the enthusiastic layperson. The British Isles offers an extraordinary historical tapestry. If ancient sites do not appeal to the imagination, we have a wealth of churches, ruined abbeys, Roman villas and medieval towns. These too have a history. Dennis Briggs, a retired engineer specialises in dowsing at church sites. He uses dowsing to detect underground archaeological features. It is not uncommon for a church to have been altered in a long period of history. New floors are laid on older ones, architectural features become hidden as improvements are implemented. Briggs has surveyed 44 church sites. Not all sites have been validated through excavation, as this is not always possible. Excavation has taken place at ten sites. Successes were recorded at St Oswald's, Durham; Hexham Chapter House; St John's, Newcastle; St Mary's, Ponteland; Woodhorn Chancel; St Mary's, Morpeth; and St Cuthbert's, Elsdon. The evaluation made by the archaeologist Professor Richard Bailey concluded by stating: 'We therefore favour an optimistic assessment of dowsing's potential as an archaeological tool for very practical reasons within church archaeology. It offers the possibility of recovering information which will not be accessible in any other way.' (*Dowsing and Church Archaeology*).

Every dowser develops an individual approach to the task in hand. Briggs describes his method: 'My method of exploring a church is to walk along its axis from west to east, noting any cross walls and putting down markers. These cross walls are tested for straightness and length, being careful to test for the possible curve of apses especially, towards the east end.' He gives the following guidelines: 'The dowser holds the rods so that the longer limbs are free to rotate in a horizontal plane and advances slowly with the longer limbs pointing forward in a questioning position. On passing over the interface between an object and its surroundings the rods swing inwards through 90 degrees. At this point the vertical limb of the

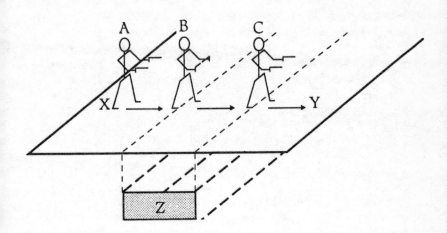

angle rods point down to the interface. On crossing the interface the rods return to the initial forward position.' Briggs himself says that 'it seems that a dowser can detect any subsurface feature which is different from its surrounding and the interfaces or boundaries are usually signalled by the movement of a hand-held device.'

Professor Bailey is not the only archaeologist to give dowsing a favourable report. In *Field Archaeology in Britain*, John Coles indicates a cooperation between archaeology and dowsing. 'At Pitnacree in Perthshire, dowsing suggested that a barrow was not encircled by a ditch and that the barrow had been placed upon a low gravel bank in the otherwise sandy terrace of the Tay; the edges of the gravel were detected by dowsing. Both suggestions were confirmed by excavation.' He noted too that dowsers are sensitive to the geological composition of differing underground features. 'Dowsers appear able to detect the presence of metals, and differences in superficial geological deposits. There is no doubt that buried ditches can be discovered by this method.'

Briggs is plainly not the only person to have used dowsing to discover underground features. In the 1970s Russian officials were reconstructing the battlefield site at Borodino. The site had been ploughed up and trees had been planted in some parts. It was known that at the time of the 1812 battle, the defending Russian army had dug a network of deep pits 100 metres in front of their guns. These defensive pits were known as wolf-holes. The authorities called in a successful dowser, Alexander Pluzhnikov. Pluzhnikov had already scored some considerable success. He had located the foundations of a fifteenth century monastery and located a series of underground tunnels and caves in the old city of Serphivok. At Borodino he was remarkably accurate in locating wolf holes. He also located a number of French graves which probably belonged to senior commanders. All the men had been neatly buried with their feet pointing north.

Dowsing has been used more recently to locate tunnels. In this instance the tunnels were those built by the Viet Cong. The hard-pressed Robert McNamara appealed for new ideas. Louis Matacia, a land surveyor, suggested dowsing, which he duly demonstrated. The

military were either suitably impressed or suitably desperate. *The New York Times* reported that engineer units of the 1st and 3rd US Marine Divisions were using L Rods to detect tunnels and caves with 'marked success'. In 1967 *The Observer*, a weekly Saigon paper for the forces, reported that 'Matacia Wire Rudders' were being used by Marines of the 2nd Battalion, 5th Marine Regiment: 'Private First Class Don R Steiner from Shadyside, Ohio, a battalion scout with the 2nd Battalion 1st Marine Regiment, tried the rods for the first time on a recent patrol. The rods spread apart as Steiner passed a Vietnamese hut. Upon checking inside the building, the Marines discovered a tunnel that led to a family bunker underneath the trail, exactly where the rods had reacted.'

The earth truly seems to have many mysteries. If you want to explore them for yourself, go outside and make a start.

## PRACTICE QUESTIONS FOR CHAPTER 5

- What were stone circles and megaliths originally used for?
- What tools or pieces of equipment would be useful at a sacred site?
- How can you use dowsing to find out about the past?
- What is a 'black stream'?
- How can dowsing be used in church sites?

# 6 IN THE GARDEN

*Now shift your gaze to the edge of the treetops against the blue sky.*
*You may see a green haze around the trees.*

Barbara Brennan, Hands of Light

E dward Bach developed his unique healing remedies guided by his own intuition and simple observation of the natural world. It is not always possible for us to wander along country lanes and explore hedgerows. However, most people have a garden which is their small piece of the natural world.

A garden is alive. It is a living place where every plant and shrub is moving through its own life cycle. Everything that lives gives out an energy field. A garden is therefore a wonderful place to interact with the many life fields generated by flowers, bulbs shrubs and trees. A plant is alive. It presents a wonderful learning opportunity for you. Even a small house plant will teach you something.

## EXERCISE 1 – happy house plants

### TECHNIQUE: DIRECT DOWSING

P lants have a great deal to teach us about the dowsing process. Begin to explore the life energy of plants in a very simple way. Take a plant. A house plant is clearly the most convenient. Hold the pendulum above the plant. Experiment to find the optimum height. If you are too far away from the plant, you will be outside its energy field and get no response. Formulate a simple question: 'Let my dowsing response, show me the life force of the plant.' Record the

dowsing response. Focus your mind on the health of the plant. When your pendulum begins to show a response, note its shape and size.

- How did the pendulum move in relation to the plant?

- What size was the circumference of the gyration in relation to the circumference of the plant?

- What do you assess the state of health to be of the plant at the time in which you conducted your dowsing experiment?

- Are you able to dowse just a single leaf? This is possible if the plant is large.

Barbara Brennan, who has a highly developed inner vision, sees the energy field of both people and plants. If you want to develop your own ability to see the living energy of the plant, she suggests in *Hands of Light*: 'Put the plant under bright lights with a dark background behind it. You may see the lines of bluegreen suddenly flashing up the plant along the leaves in the direction of growth. The colour slowly fades, only to flash again, perhaps on the opposite side of the plant. These lines will react to your hand, or a piece of crystal, if you bring them near the aura of the plants.'

Remove a leaf from your plant. Dowse it at regular intervals.

- How long does it take for the leaf to lose its energy?

- Do you think the same time scale will apply to all plants? What factors might influence this process?

- Dowse the place where you have taken the leaf from. Do you detect anything unusual at this point?

When you have experimented with one house plant, try another, preferably one of a different size. Compare the response from both plants. What have you learned from this simple experiment? What have you discovered about your plants? Hopefully your house plants are healthy, in which case you will have obtained a positive steady gyration. If your plant is not doing as well as it might, you will have discovered a negative reaction. When you feel confident,

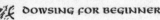 
go out into your garden and begin to explore the energy reactions of your plants.

## EXERCISE 2 – The flower Bed

### Technique: Direct Dowsing

You may need a bigger pendulum to work with larger plants. I have a large crystal droplet on a cord for outside work. Experiment with a single shrub at first. Keep focused on the health of the plant. If you have a small border, you can move quite easily from one plant to another. This simple exercise is very revealing. My garden is quite small with just two borders and a collection of tubs. I gave my garden the once over recently. Moving swiftly over each plant, I was pleased to get a positive reaction throughout my first border. Along the second border, I dowsed over two shrubs which were rather close together. One was thriving, but clearly at the expense of the other. One gave me a positive reaction, a gyration, the other gave me a negative reaction. For me this shows as an oscillation. I moved on to my patio tubs where all was well, with the exception of one small shrub clearly not enjoying the confines of the pot. I moved both plants on the basis of my finding with the pendulum. If you do this regularly you won't see your garden in the same light again.

# The Living Tree

*The names of the letters in the modern Irish alphabet are also those of trees.*

Robert Graves, The White Goddess

Trees have their own folklore and mythology. Certain trees are considered to be lucky, others unlucky. Different woods of course have quite different properties. In the ancient world, trees generally were regarded as sacred. We have replaced the concept of the sacred grove with that of pure utilitarianism. The resulting

deforestation threatens us all. So when we encounter a tree, we might rediscover something of the respect shown by previous generations, who lived in harmony with nature. Lethbridge became interested in trees after a chance remark by his wife: 'Why do you think that some trees are considered to be unlucky?' Lethbridge set about his self-appointed task in his own typical fashion. His curiosity was aroused. Bearing the folklore of trees in mind, he cut pieces of elder, rowan, oak, holly and elm. He collected samples from 14 trees in all, and as might be expected Lethbridge made a bizarre discovery. Of his 14 samples, six, the elder, ash, elm, holly, fig and pine, each responded to the rate of 24 inches, the rate for maleness. The remaining eight samples from the rowan, oak, thorn, hazel, willow, apple, ivy and beech, all responded to the 29 inch rate for femaleness. He also found that rowan had a very peculiar property: it served as an interrupter like lead. According to folklore, rowan holds a rather special place: it was used as a protection against witchcraft. Rowan trees were planted beside farmsteads, and rowan branches were nailed above doorways. Pigs were even given collars of rowan. Lethbridge was bemused by his own findings and said, 'From a botanical view this was all nonsense.' However, there is more to trees than just botany. If your curiosity too is aroused, you might make some discoveries for yourself.

## EXERCISE 3 – LIVING TREES

### TECHNIQUE: DIRECT DOWSING

If you have successfully located the energy field from a small house plant, expand your horizons and attempt to encounter the energy field radiated by a tree. Using L Rods or a natural Y Rod, walk slowly towards a tree. How close can you get before you experience a reaction? Try to approach the tree from all sides, as this will give you a better idea of how far the energy field of the tree extends. If possible try this on more than one tree. How does this relate to the size and age of the tree?

## EXERCISE 4 – LEAVES AND BRANCHES

### TECHNIQUE: DIRECT DOWSING

Collect samples from differing trees, you will only need a small sample.

- Use a long pendulum. Are you able to detect either the 24 or the 29 inch rate for your samples?

- Devise an experiment of your own to test the properties of the rowan tree.

- Find out how various trees have been depicted in folklore. Can you make a correlation between the mythological qualities and the responses that you discover through the pendulum?

- Can you devise an experiment of your own, in the light of your reading?

# The four seasons

The gardening year is the seasonal year. Might we detect seasonal differences in the activity of plants and trees?

## Spring

Spring is of course the time for phenomenal growth. The first green haze of new life on the trees always lifts our spirits. The appearance of spring bulbs tells us that winter is over. But what is happening at the unseen and invisible levels? It was Burr who discovered that the energy field radiated by a seed was a good indication of its future growth. It would be difficult to dowse over small individual seeds. However, we may transfer the same principle to the springtime seedling collection.

## EXERCISE 5 – THE SEEDTRAY

### TECHNIQUE: DIRECT DOWSING

Check your seedlings with a pendulum. When they are potted on, what reaction do you get as they settle into new surroundings? Check at regular intervals: you might be surprised by what you can learn about the time it takes for plants to adjust to being moved. Be aware of any plants that give you a consistently negative reaction. Compare their growth with those that show a positive reaction from the start.

## SUMMER

Summer is the time of fruition. The seedlings have matured. The garden is full of colour. There is plenty for the gardener to do in the garden and the greenhouse.

## EXERCISE 6 – IN THE GREENHOUSE

### TECHNIQUE: DIRECT DOWSING

There are endless opportunities for experimenting. The different stages of a plant's growth provide many opportunities to correlate a dowsing response with a recognisable condition.

- Dowse when you know that a plant is dry and in need of water. What do you discover?

- Dowse if you notice that a plant has been attacked by pests. What do you discover?

- Dowse when you recognise that a plant looks absolutely perfect. What do you discover?

## AUTUMN

After the glorious display of the summer, comes the autumn. At this time of the year the energies are subsiding. Can we gain a deeper

understanding of the cyclic nature of plant life by dowsing through the seasons?

- Dowse your shrubs when they are pruned. What do you discover?

- Dowse any spectacular bulbs. What do you detect as those flowers die back?

- Dowse a sample of autumnal leaves. What do you detect?

## WINTER

- Can you detect any differences between the life fields of evergreens and deciduous trees?

- Can you detect any difference in the life field of plants that need to overwinter and those that are hardy?

- What happens to the life field of a plant that has been frostbitten?

## EXERCISE 7 – THE SICK BED

### TECHNIQUE: INDIRECT DOWSING

If you discover a reading which shows that the plant is not thriving, you might like to dowse for a possible solution. Hold your pendulum over the plant while focusing on each question in turn. If you are an experienced gardener you may well expand your questions. Write out a basic check list. For instance:

- Does this plant need more water?

- Does this plant need less water?

- Does this plant need food?

- Does this plant need moving?

Plants do not thrive if the soil lacks the appropriate nutrients. Whitlock suggests the following procedure for checking the

relationship between soil and plant. Place any part of the plant on a board. On the same surface, place a sample of soil taken from where the plant has been growing. In one hand hold the pendulum. Take a wooden skewer in the other hand. Hold the pendulum over the soil; hold the skewer as pointer over the plant. According to Whitlock, he experiences an oscillation followed by one of the following four reactions:

- The oscillations increase – the soil and sample are compatible.

- The oscillations continue with little change – the plant can tolerate the soil.

- The oscillation changes to a clockwise rotation – the soil is deficient.

- The oscillation changes to an anticlockwise rotation – a deficiency in the soil, which cannot be rectified.

In the case of a soil deficiency, Whitlock adds a little trace element while still holding the pendulum over the plant and the pointer over the soil until the pendulum again takes up an oscillation. This system clearly worked for him. You might like to try the procedure for yourself. Remember you will need to be clear about your own code.

Whitlock also followed the idea that certain plants benefit from being planted together. He devised a test for this too: 'Set the two plants to be tested on a flat surface, about 25 inches apart. The pendulum is held over one plant, the pointer is directed over the other. When the pendulum starts to oscillate, move it towards the second plant. If the oscillations increase in strength, the two plants are highly compatible. If the oscillations show little change, the two plants are tolerant or indifferent to each other. If the oscillations switch to gyrations the two are repelled by each other. The stronger the gyrations, or if they are anticlockwise, the greater the antipathy.'

He discovered that garlic and beetroot are attracted to each other, but garlic and roses are repelled. There are plenty of plants that you can test for yourself.

# Mysteries in the garden

The garden is a living place. Nature has her own mysteries.
Lethbridge always loved a mystery. He made some interesting and
quite bizarre discoveries through dowsing experiments. He was a
profoundly curious man. One evening in 1964, he found a dead
beetle. It had flown through an open window and landed in a
glucose drink. Lethbridge recognised the beetle and wondered where
it had been feeding in the locality. When he discovered that the
beetle fed on truffles, and not on dung as he originally believed, he
set out to dig for truffles. However, he did not go about his search in
quite the usual manner. He purchased a tin of paté containing a tiny
slice of truffle and assessed its rate. He found that the truffle
responded to two rates, one of 21 inches, the rate shared by other
fungi, and 17 inches, its own rate. Armed with only this piece of
information, he set out for the local woods with a pointer in one
hand and a pendulum in the other. Several spots were indicated but
they were difficult to reach. Finally, he records, in *Ghost and
Divining Rod*: 'We began to move the old beech leaves with a
trowel. We took them away and began to scrape off the earth
beneath. Perhaps three inches from the original surface, there was a
small spherical object. It was about the size of a large green pea,
and the colour of dried blood. We thought that it must be some kind
of truffle. It was obviously a fungus: but we had never seen anything
like it before. It was harder than a puff ball.' The strange sample was
sent away to the South Kensington museum. A letter was duly
returned which stated that the fungus was indeed the foodstuff of
the beetle, *bolboceras*. Moreover, both beetle and fungus were rare.
Winter set in and he had to abandon the search, but when
conditions permitted Lethbridge was back on the trail again. Using
the long pendulum set at the 17 inch rate which he had established
for truffle, he returned to the woods. Using his usual searching
procedure he localised a target area. However he did not find truffle.
'Exactly beneath the central point of the circle was the caterpillar,
the larva of a beetle of the chafer family to which *bolboceras*
belongs. In looking for the truffle, I had found a beetle grub with a
truffle's pendulum rate and no truffle.'

Lethbridge continued his off-beat experiments and discovered that the beetle, the truffle on which it fed, the beech tree where the truffles were found and the beech nuts which grew upon the tree all responded to the 17 inch rate. What can we make of this? Even the snail *cyclostoma elegans*, which feeds under the beech tree, responded to the 17 inch rate. Lethbridge's interest in the natural world never ceased. He was interested in how birds followed migration routes and how insects found their food. He was only able to hypothesise about the principles behind migration, but he was able to set up some practical dowsing experiments between insects and their food supplies. He tested the dung beetles *aphodius rufipes, ater fimitarius* and *erraticus*. They all responded to a 16 inch rate, as did cow dung. He tested ten species of *chrysomela*. Each had the same rate as its specialised plant food. The best intentions of gardeners are thwarted by the actions of insect hordes. The question of how insects locate their food has important practical implications for gardeners. Whitlock also investigated this relationship. He found that many traditional old wives tales about companion planting were upheld. The gardener might therefore use planting consciously to defend the garden. You can experiment for yourself using the procedures already described by Whitlock. He discovered that honey bees like lemon balm and that aphids are attracted to roses but repelled by nasturtiums and nettles. Ants and the cabbage white butterfly are repelled by mint. Carrot fly are repelled by onions.

It would seem then that old wives tales and traditional folklore embody truths about the natural world. In an age desperately attempting to redefine our relationship to the natural world, we might employ dowsing to show us what our five senses cannot detect. So, work hand in hand with Nature and discover at least some of her mysteries.

# 7 DOWSING FOR FUN

*A practised dowser tends to find only what he seeks.*
Dennis Briggs, Dowsing and Church Archaeology

Dowsing is fun. It should never be dull. You can be as experimental as your imagination and skill will permit. You can employ your dowsing skill for the most mundane tasks or for the most esoteric investigations. Every experiment should be a learning process. Even so called 'failures' have something to teach.

You may find that you have an aptitude for one kind of dowsing. Perhaps you relate really well to plant life but don't have much success with dowsing for electrical faults, or perhaps you have a high rate of success with electrical equipment but just seem to lack those green fingers. Develop those skills which show signs of immediate success. Refine your experiments. Become really adventurous, set yourself increasingly more difficult challenges. This chapter is meant to awaken your imagination but don't be limited by the suggestions. Dowsing can be a real learning process. Every dowsing experience, no matter how small, should make you think about yourself and the world in which you live. It may change the view that you have of yourself.

There is no doubt that successful dowsing is related to a unity between the conscious and unconscious mind. Dowsing itself creates a bridge between the conscious and unconscious mind, so the more often you dowse, the more this link is strengthened. This unification process may have beneficial results.

We may identify the rational and deductive mental processes with the functions of the left-hand side of the brain, and the creative inspirational and irrational processes with the functions of the right-hand side. This does not mean that consciousness is located in the left side and the unconscious in the right – only that the two hemispheres correspond to these twin aspects. Maxwell Cade's invention, the Mind Mirror, has enabled us to see the activity of these hemispheres and is possibly the ultimate biofeedback machine, showing us the very patterns created by our own thoughts. It translates the different brain patterns into a light display. So far, four quite separate brain rhythms have been distinguished. Each is associated with a certain kind of mental activity. The alpha rhythm is commonly found in the relaxed but alert state of mind. The beta rhythm is associated with concentration and externally focused attention. The theta and delta rhythms are less commonly found and are observed in deep states of meditation, implicated in the healing exchange and other related phenomena. The machine has been used in various situations often with both meditators and dowsers. The Mind Mirror actually shows us the dowser's mind in action. Bill Lewis assisted the Dragon Project in its research. He was wired up to the Mind Mirror as he dowsed at the Rollright Stones and showed both theta and delta brain patterns.

The Mind Mirror has also been used with great effect to train people in meditative techniques which harmonise the two sides of the brain, bringing conscious and subconscious together in balance. Jung stressed the importance of the whole being, stressing that personhood could not be achieved without a balance between these two halves. The Mind Mirror shows us the effect of the all too common one-sided development, an incomplete person.

Dowsing is a wonderfully irrational practice. It draws upon abilities that we have lost and on faculties that we don't understand, and this should be celebrated not undermined. Rationality by itself is truly sterile. We need the voice of the unconscious too. As the bridge between the two levels of being is constructed, we create change in ourselves. This in turn brings another faculty into play, namely intuition. It is no surprise that, for some, dowsing opens the door to spiritual growth. Indeed dowsing should contribute to personal growth, for it draws upon the very qualities reflected by materialist

society. Others will strenuously deny such possibilities and will want to understand dowsing only as a muscular reflex. However, everyone is free to take from dowsing what they can. Dowsing is a method of exploring, so let's explore.

## EXERCISE 1 – SEARCHING

### TECHNIQUE: DIRECT DOWSING

This is the old fashioned 'Kim's Game' with a difference. Gather a good selection of small objects made from various materials: keys, pencil, pile of staples, coin, piece of wood, crystal etc. Get a friend to arrange them on a tray and cover it with a cloth.

- How many can objects can you find by dowsing?

- How might you differentiate between the various substances, wood and metal for instance? Is it possible to establish a code using the number of gyrations for each substance?

- What can you learn about each substance underneath the cover?

Try the same technique on a larger scale. Ask a friend to hide things beneath a blanket or under a rug. When you have had some success at this, you will be more confident about searching for buried things, which are in essence buried under a blanket of earth. Digging up the countryside is not to be advised, though you can always dig up your own back garden with impunity. You might like to use the network of cables and pipes beneath every street as a training exercise. Can you follow a pipe along your road?

I was once asked to dowse for a client. Ostensibly I was being asked to run a chakra profile, but it turned out to be a searching exercise. Before my daughter was born I ran a hypnotherapy practice for a couple of years. I did not always confine myself to straightforward hypnotherapy. A young man came to me. He had reached a point where his existing belief structure was failing to help him in his day to day life and, most crucially, in his job. He was a military forensic scientist. We spoke about many life issues. I had touched upon life

energies and dowsing. He was sceptical, critical and questioning. In
true empirical fashion, he wanted proof and asked if I was willing to
give him a personal demonstration on his terms. I agreed, on the
grounds that he couldn't expect anything too spectacular or bizarre.
He came fully prepared at our next meeting. I had previously
explained how I might dowse over the body for signs of ill health.
He asked if I would dowse over him. This seemed like a reasonable
request. I dowsed in the usual manner and reported back to him as I
did so. I located some unexpected readings which did not conform
to the usual pattern around the heart and central abdomen. I merely
reported that these areas were giving unusual and distorted
readings. He looked at me quizzically and proceeded to unbutton
his shirt. Taped to his chest was a bullet; taped to his abdomen was
a metal crucifix.

## EXERCISE 2 – WHERE IS IT?

### TECHNIQUE: INDIRECT DOWSING

Dowsing can be used to search for an object. All searching
exercises are essentially the same. You need to focus on the
missing object, whether you are looking for house keys or a glove.
Try to get a clear mental picture of what you are looking for.
Physically dowsing for an object is a good training exercise, but it is
not always practical, especially if you really have no idea where to
begin your search. You might instead begin by narrowing down your
field of search by asking, 'Is the missing object to be found in the
hall?' etc. You can go through a list of possible locations one at a
time. When you get a positive response, rephrase your question.
You can then try a physical dowsing search or simply go back to
that place and look very carefully.

There is nothing more frustrating than not being able to find
something that you need. One summer my husband had gone to
help a friend erect a fence. Late in the morning I got a phone call
saying that they had been stalled for the last hour. They had
managed to lose a small but vital screwdriver. My husband asked if

I could use dowsing to help and although I thought this was rather a tall order I said I would try.

I drew a map of the garden, which I knew quite well, and divided it into a grid. I went through each grid asking if the screwdriver was present. Unfortunately I seemed to get rather contradictory responses, as my pendulum gave me positive responses in more than one place. I had failed, and could not give a definite answer, and I felt I had not been of great help. I must admit I was a bit annoyed at this failure. Before giving up completely I opened up to plain insight by concentrating on the screwdriver and then being aware of any response. The only image that appeared in my mind was of darkness, and I deduced that they might well have buried it by mistake. I rang up with my tale of failure, wished them luck and went back to what I had been doing. The phone rang some time later. They had found the screwdriver – not under the earth as I had wrongly deduced, but in our friend's back pocket. Well it was certainly dark in there!

## EXERCISE 3 – TUNING IN

### TECHNIQUE: DIRECT DOWSING

The long pendulum is especially useful at direct search procedures. You will need to utilise the table of rates. Set your pendulum cord at the length suggested and see if you are as successful as Lethbridge at this type of work. He found silver coins, seventeenth century pottery, a brass tag from a lace and many other historical items. Lethbridge recorded many instances when he was staggered by his own success. 'The pendulum was absurdly accurate. The field of force around each object may be small, for it can be pinpointed underground within six inches; but the human field must be widely extensible, for I had located the three objects at a distance of two or three yards. You have only to take the pendulum to the place you want to search, adjust the length of the cord for the metal you wish to find and swing the ball and point with the left hand. When the back and forward motion change to a circular swing, you have located your quarry.' You should never be bored if you master even one of the searching techniques.

## EXERCISE 4 – CRYSTALS

### TECHNIQUE: DIRECT DOWSING

C rystals are very popular these days. Everyone is magnetised by their beauty. Each crystal has its own unique structure. Most people seem to have a crystal or two these days. This would seem to be a very interesting avenue for the amateur dowser. I became interested in this question myself recently and I began to dowse over various crystals. I have to say that I saw a reaction that I never witnessed before. I am obviously familiar with circles of various strengths, both clockwise and anticlockwise, horizontal oscillations and even the standstill, but when I dowsed the crystal the response can only be described as a star. The pendulum traced a series of straight lines, while at the same time describing a circle, the end result being a star configuration. I was interested to discover a new response after all these years. I do feel that some interesting research might be carried out here. See what you can discover for yourself.

- Can you detect any difference between various crystals?

- Do you find any difference between a crystal that is regularly used for healing and one that is pristine?

- Experiment with a long pendulum. Can you detect a rate for different crystals?

- What response do you get from a collection of crystals, of the same type and from differing types?

- Do you discover any conflicts between crystals of different types?

## EXERCISE 5 – WHICH CRYSTAL?

### TECHNIQUE: INDIRECT DOWSING

T here are many beautiful crystals. Each crystal has its own properties and characteristics. If you are thinking of choosing a

crystal to use for your own growth, why not use dowsing to help you select what you need? Use a list of crystals and go through it in the usual way. Ask, 'Does this crystal have something to offer me?' Use this short list to start you off.

| | |
|---|---|
| Iron pyrite | Yellow citrine |
| Tiger eye | Violet tourmaline |
| Garnet | Amethyst |
| Agate | Rose quartz |

Dowse again to assess which qualities might be developed for you. Ask, 'Will this crystal help me to develop my sense of . . .'

| | |
|---|---|
| Being grounded | Initiating activity |
| Feeling calm | Opening to spiritual development |
| Experiencing warmth | Generating love |

Crystals form a fascinating subject in their own right. Perhaps you can deepen your own interest and understanding by incorporating dowsing in your work with crystals.

# SACRED OBJECTS

I have gathered a collection of artefacts over the years. Some have been given to me, others have been chosen and bought by me. I have quite a collection, representing the many religious traditions of the world, both past and present. Recently I was given a very beautiful and charming statuette of an Egyptian goddess. Unusually it is made from cast metal. It has been hand painted with great delicacy. As it is new it has been handled very little. On a whim I decided, to dowse over this latest acquisition. The pendulum moved quickly into a large and strong clockwise circle which was far bigger than the circumference of the rather slim statuette. I felt that the response was a reflection, not of the metal used to make the statuette, but of the care lavished upon it by the maker. I became interested in the dowsing response to crafted works, and began to explore the reaction of the artefacts. I dowsed a *djore* in my possession. This is a Tibetan symbol, representing the lightning bolt, which I had bought at the Tibetan exhibition in London. As soon as

I began to dowse I was aware of an extraordinarily powerful response. The pendulum began to whiz around in a clockwise circle, moving so fast that under its own speed it rose higher and higher. I tried dowsing on several occasions and the pendulum performed in exactly the same way. By this time I was quite fascinated by these experiences. I then dowsed over a statuette of Bast, the Egyptian cat. This statuette is by now a classic representation of Bast and is often reproduced. This particular statuette came from the British Museum; it was bought as a gift for me. The pendulum reacted with an idle and almost lifeless swing backwards and forwards. The response was neither a circle nor an oscillation, but a pathetically slow wobble.

My simple experiments made me think a great deal about sacred art in general, and I began to wonder about all the Egyptian statues in museums, all the Tibetan statues in monasteries and all the icons in churches. Now you may not have a collection of statuettes to experiment with, but it seems to me that the key factor here is the intention of the maker. Both my Egyptian and Tibetan statuettes revealed a great vitality but the mass produced item was totally lifeless. Lethbridge was also interested in how items seemed to retain an imprint from its maker. He tested an original drawing and compared it with a reproduction. The original showed both a 24 inch rate, indicating that its creator was male, and a 27 inch rate, indicating thought. However, the reproductions showed neither. Lethbridge refined this interest even further and began to test exclusively to see whether he might be able to detect the sex of the original artist. He began to test original paintings that came his way and claimed to be able to pick up either the 24 or the 29 inch rate.

You might therefore have a little fun dowsing any hand-crafted items that you might have. You may have a hand-thrown piece of pottery, a model lovingly given by one of your children, or grandma's handmade tablecloth. You might also try an object that has been constantly handled by one person, such as a well-loved favourite tool or a piece of jewellery. Dowsing in this way tends to confirm that quite ordinary objects can reveal something about their creators or owners. Psychometry is a particular psychic gift. Those blessed with this ability hold a given object and tune in to it. Perhaps many

of the objects around us are in truth imbued with the care and attention shown to them over many years. Dowse for yourself and see what you can discover about the simple objects in your own home and family.

## EXERCISE 6 – WHO MADE IT?

### TECHNIQUE: DIRECT DOWSING

Take the object that you are interested in, dowse directly over the object to see what response you get. Use a long pendulum. Can you detect the male rate of 24 inches, or the female rate of 29 inches? Can you detect a 27 inch rate indicating thought? Are you able to detect any emotional qualities? How would you test an object for anger?

## EXERCISE 7 – FAMILY HISTORY

### TECHNIQUE: INDIRECT DOWSING

Try asking questions about the object. If you are dowsing with a family heirloom you will obviously try and personalise your questions. Perhaps there are some areas of family history you might like to explore. Use the long pendulum to test for the gender of the originator if this is relevant. Remember you can dowse for dates too. Try getting information about the history of the object.

- Was this object made in (name countries)?

- Was this object made in the . . . (name century)?

Lethbridge was also interested in the relationship between an object and a person. As part of his archaeological work he visited some excavations at an iron age camp at Pilsdon Pen in Dorset, where he picked up a collection of pebbles clearly gathered from the local beach to be used as sling shot. He tested them with the pendulum and found one reading for flint, one for thought and one for the rate

associated by Lethbridge with 'male'. As a test group he gathered another collection from the beach with tongs. These gave rates for flint and for thought, but did not react to the male rate. He picked up a pebble and threw it at the wall with great ferocity. When the same pebble was tested, it now registered the male rate. Pebbles thrown in the same way by his wife registered the female rate after being handled. He tested stones which he also believed had been used as sling shot from another hill site. These, too, registered the rate for silica, 14, the rate for thought, 27 and the rate for 'male', 24.

# (D)ap dowsing

*It strains one's imagination to believe that a paperclip on the end of a cotton thread can tell us the location of underground streams in the Australian outback.*

DM Lewis

Lewis was himself a dowser so he understood the credibility gap at first hand. However, when the imagination is strained to breaking point it is clearly time to enlarge the world view which serves to constrain us. When I started college I had some time in which to further my interest in all things metaphysical. I simply found practical dowsing to be great fun. I was always devising new situations to test myself, and I was especially interested to assess the role of the mind as a means of tuning in to an object or quality. I tested this out in many ways. I used to cut out squares of paper, write numbers on the back, turn them over, spread them out and search for a chosen number. The results were sporadic but interesting. I was sometimes successful, but not always. An extremely high success rate would have been quite extraordinary. As an extension of this idea, I decided one day to try my luck at map dowsing with a difference. I experimented over maps, particularly over areas marked as lakes or rivers. However, as I was not in a position to follow up my dowsing with any field work, I decided to search for a landmark, 'blind'. I went to a draw where I had a collection of maps and took what I took to be a map covering the area where I used to live. I spread the map out on the table face down, and decided to dowse to find Sevenoaks Road, where I had lived as a child. This entailed dowsing over the back of the map in small sections and noting both positive and negative reactions while keeping the thought clearly in my mind. I seemed to get repeated positive responses in one place only. I turned the map over and discovered that I had picked up the wrong map. I had been dowsing over a map of Kent, not SE London. Then I burst out laughing. I had located the town of Sevenoaks in Kent, not Sevenoaks Road!

All anecdotal evidence from dowsers follows the same pattern and each dowser offers a rather embarrassed apology to the reader, after all dowsing from a map makes no sense whatsoever but dowsers are eminently practical folk who always know that the proof of the pudding is in the eating. They cannot help but try this crazy sounding system for themselves and are even more embarrassed when it functions perfectly well.

In his book, *Water Divining*, Whitlock describes his first attempt at map dowsing: 'I started with a locality I knew well, my own house and its environs, and checked the underground streams I knew existed from previous explorations with the dowsing rod. In my left hand I took a pointer, one of those wooden meat skewers, and between my thumb and forefingers of my right hand I held a short pendulum, not over the map but over the bare table beside it. I placed the tip of the pointer near the house and moved slowly towards what I knew to be the lines of an underground stream. When it responded, the pendulum, which had been gently oscillating, began to gyrate.' This started Whitlock dowsing in an entirely new field. When he was approached to dowse for water in a drought ridden area of Portugal he did so with success.

Whitlock favours the use of a pointer, which worked well for him. He uses the pointer to move across the map while holding the pendulum to the side of the map. Using the grid as markers, he checks each square one at a time.

There are of course many possibilities. Everyone must find a system which suits them. Whitlock also suggests drawing a line on the map

and asking; 'Is it on this line?' Lonegren uses L Rods in a unique way for map dowsing. He holds them upside down and the system works perfectly well for him.

Map dowsing is not confined to dowsing for water. Thomas Trench was contacted by the Belgian police to find the body of someone killed in the Brussels riots in 1966 and then taken away by the murderers. Trench took a photograph of them and a small scale map of Belgium. His pendulum reacted to a spot near Blankenberghe. He then worked on a large scale map of this area and identified the position of the body within some fifty yards.

Why not have a go yourself? You have nothing to lose and maybe something to learn.

## EXERCISE 8 – WHERE IS IT?

### TECHNIQUE: INDIRECT DOWSING

Take a large scale map. Become familiar with the map and try to visualise the scenery as you move across the various sections. What happens to the pendulum when you pass over water on the map, such as a lake or river? Do you have a map which shows the location of an ancient stone site? What happens when you cross this spot? Map dowsing is often combined with a search of some kind, whether for water or a missing person. You will need to formulate the relevant question and then apply it to each section of the map noting the response of the pendulum each time. You might like to try using a pointer as Whitlock suggests. However, ultimately you will need to devise your own system. To give you some confidence, take a large scale map of your local area. Give yourself a target. What is to be identified does not matter so long as you know the answer. You are attempting to access a new level of sensitivity within yourself. Clearly the map depicts many features, both natural and man-made, that might attract your attention. You need to focus your awareness so that the pendulum responds only to features consciously selected by you.

A map, of course, is a two-dimensional representation of a three-dimensional reality. As you become more familiar with map reading, you can visualise the landscape and scenery in your mind's eye. This will help you become attuned to the site as a whole.

- Can you locate the local school, church, railway line, nearest source of water?

- Can you detect any large underground features such as tunnels or caves?

- Can you distinguish geological differences? See if you can differentiate between chalk, clay, granite, slate etc.

Choose a map of a different district. Now you have no subconscious information to help you.

- Search for water.

- Search for different geological strata.

- Search for tunnels or large underground cavities.

Make an effort to check your results by looking into the history and geography of the area which you have chosen. Perhaps you will be able to put these skills to good use at some time.

Finally I offer you two applications that you might like to try for yourself.

## EXERCISE 9 – WHEN WAS I BORN?

### TECHNIQUE: INDIRECT DOWSING

The moment of birth is special. It marks our entry into the world. An accurate time is really required if we want to have a horoscope cast. Yet for a variety of reasons and circumstances many people simply do not know the time of their birth. If you are in this category you might like to try a simple and harmless bit of fun.

You simply need to make a list of the hours a.m. and p.m. Go through the list an hour at a time using your pendulum. Focus your mind on a question such as 'Was I born near this hour?' Go through the list recording your responses, you may find a positive result for more than one time. I think that this is because birth is often a protracted event. For example, the pendulum may respond in a positive way to the hours 2 a.m. and 3 a.m. but responds negatively to 4 a.m. This would indicate that birth took place not much earlier than 2 a.m. and no later than 4 a.m. So now we refine our response by dowsing for the minutes. It is quite sufficient to make a list covering five-minute periods. Write down intervals of five minutes. Dowse each one asking a clear question, 'was I born between 2 a.m. and 2.05 a.m.?' Continue through the intervals noting the response each time. I have used this technique on several occasions and it does seem to yield interesting results. I have then gone on to prepare charts based on the time of birth as assessed by the pendulum and the resulting charts have shown a very positive likeness.

# The electric current

I have to admit that I know less about electricity than I do about dowsing. However, I discovered quite by chance that it is possible to check electrical connections through dowsing. My husband had come home with a brand new keyboard for the computer. He duly connected it and nothing happened. He put this down to a faulty product and took it back to the office. He came home the next night with another keyboard, which he also duly connected, and again nothing happened. This time, however, tempers wore a little thin. As a last resort I offered to see if I could help. Until that very moment I had never dowsed anything electrical. I dowsed over the lead from the keyboard into the computer and this gave a positive reading. Next I dowsed over the lead from the keyboard itself. I told him my results. He turned the keyboard over and there at the base of the keyboard was a small switch which he had forgotten to turn on!

## EXERCISE 10 – WHERE'S THE FAULT?

### TECHNIQUE: DIRECT DOWSING

There are plenty of electrical appliances in every house. Try dowsing over a lead when the appliance is plugged in. Try again when it is not plugged in. Can you detect a difference?

There are lots of ways of using dowsing in everyday life. I expect that you can discover some that I've never even thought of. Don't forget, practice makes perfect. Have fun.

---

**PRACTICE QUESTIONS FOR CHAPTERS 6–7**

- How can your garden help you to practise your dowsing?

- How can you use the four seasons to experiment?

- What is the Mind Mirror and how is it used?

- Give some practical applications for using dowsing in everyday situations at home.

- How can map dowsing be used?

- How can dowsing help you to find electrical faults?

# 8 BEYOND THE PENDULUM

*We are dealing with matters which are evidently perfectly simple to the sixth sense, but incredible to the others.*

TC Lethbridge, A Step in the Dark

Successful dowsing constantly shows us the limitations of a materialistic philosophy. We have to admit that there are things we cannot explain. That dowsing works is beyond doubt, yet in truth we do not fully understand how it works. The dowsing phenomenon constantly presents us with tough challenges, most especially when it appears to defy our accepted view of reality. Lethbridge was unafraid to push back the boundaries of his own understanding. He used the pendulum to take him to metaphysical areas which are far beyond the familiar and earthy practice of plain water divining.

Lethbridge remained faithful to the idea that substances resonate at a particular rate. When he had established a number of rates to his own satisfaction, he observed certain relationships which he found interesting. He noticed that several major concepts were found at regular 10 inch intervals. He was profoundly moved by the relationship indicated between the 20 inch and 40 inch rates of life. He noted that dead organic objects reacted to both the 20 inch rate of life and the 40 inch rate, which he had assigned to both sleep and death. He concluded that the 40 inch rate represents 'life force in a higher plane'. He wrote: 'This is so remarkable that we must surely conclude that this scale was evolved by something outside our earthly three dimensions.' Here is metaphysical speculation indeed, engendered by practical experiments with pendulum, lengths of cords and assorted items both archaeological and organic.

He noted the following relationships:

- **10 inches**
  Light, sun, fire, red, east, graphite, truth.

- **20 inches**
  Life, heat, earth, white, south, electricity.

- **30 inches**
  Sound, moon, water, green, west, hydrogen.

- **40 inches**
  Death, cold, air, black, north, sleep, falsehood.

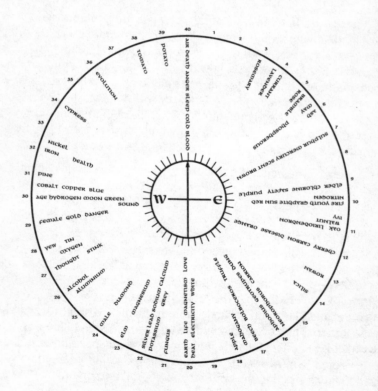

Lethbridge also became interested in abstract qualities. He tabulated these over a number of years through some very off-beat experiments.

| Rate in inches | Quality |
| --- | --- |
| 10 | Light |
| 20 | Life Force |
| 24 | Male Principle |
| 27 | Thought or memory |
| 29 | Female principle |
| 30 | Sound |
| 40 | Sleep or death |

He drew out a compass rose of rates based on 40 inch divisions. When he plotted the rates, he discovered that he had drawn a spiral. Now a spiral is of course a fundamental natural form. This made him wonder if he could record any rates beyond 40. He took sulphur, with a known rate of 7 inches, and dowsed at 47 inches (40 + 7). He also took silver, with a known rate of 22 inches, and dowsed at 62 inches (40 + 22). He expected to find nothing but instead he traced a secondary track. He began to dwell deeply on metaphysical relationships. He knew he had gone far beyond common sense: 'I am trying to present something which will make very little sense to most readers.' Yet he had encountered a puzzle and he could not bear to leave a puzzle alone.

Others too have stepped over a metaphysical threshold through dowsing. Lonegren unashamedly sees dowsing as a spiritual adventure. He uses a sevenfold model developed by Terry Ross, former President of the American Society of Dowsers. The model appeals to me as it links in with qualities which we may develop as we open the higher chakras. I have therefore adapted the model accordingly.

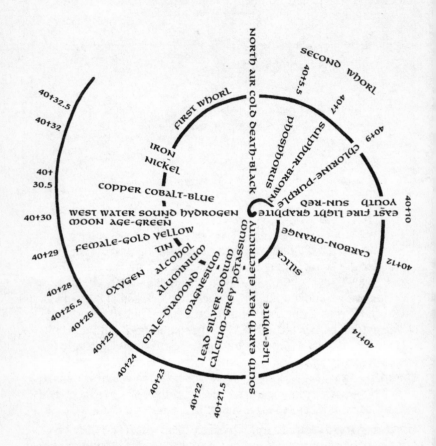

## The Seven Levels of Dowsing
### Level 1
On site field dowsing, dowsing for water.

### Level 2
Off site field work, dowsing from a distance, dowsing allied to subconscious.

**Level 3**
Dowsing expands as a means of self realisation.

**Level 4**
Desire to serve others through dowsing, distant healing.

**Level 5**
Dowsing becomes internalised, all devices can be dispensed with.

**Level 6**
Dowsing allied almost exclusively to insight and intuition.

**Level 7**
Dowser's will is aligned to the cosmic will.

We might like to contemplate these levels as we set out on the journey. Who knows where dowsing might lead us? Dowsing can take us into the heart of the mystery which is life itself. There is no power in the pendulum itself; the power lies within us. The power of a clear thought seems to defy limitation. It is no surprise then that we should close on a mystery. What arrogant fools we should be if we really believed we knew everything. Dowsing shows how much more we have to learn. Like Lethbridge, we too should thrive on curiosity.

## Useful addresses

*The British Society of Dowsers*, Sycamore Cottage, Tamley Lane, Hastingleigh, Ashford, Kent TN25 5H – has a good selection of books and dowsing implements for sale; also a good library for its members.

*The Dragon Project*, c/o Empress Box, 92 Penzance Cornwall TR18 2LX – organises practical experiments into a wide range of earth mysteries and related phenomena.

*Ilkley Healing Centre*, 7/8 Nelson Road, Ilkley, West Yorkshire LS29 8HN – centre run by Arthur Bailey; the Bailey Flower essences are obtainable.

# Further Reading

Bailey, Arthur, Cambridge & Briggs, *Dowsing and Church Archaeology*, Intercept, 1988.

Bailey, Arthur, *Dowsing for Health*, Quantum, 1990.

Brennan, Barbara Ann, *Hands of Light*, A Bantam New Age Book, 1988.

Devereux, Paul, *Earth Memory*, Quantum, Foulsham, 1991.

Graves, Tom, *The Dowser's Workbook*, The Aquarian Press, 1989.

Hitching, Francis, *Earth Magic*, Book Club Associates, 1976.

Jurriaanse, D, *The Practical Pendulum Book*, Samuel Weiser, 1986.

Lethbridge, TC, *ESP Beyond Time and Distance*, Sidgwick and Jackson, 1965.

Lethbridge, TC, *Ghost and Divining Rod*, Routledge & Kegan Paul, 1963.

Lethbridge, TC, *The Legend of the Sons of God*, Routledge & Kegan Paul, 1972.

Lonegren, Sig, *Spiritual Dowsing*, Gothic Image, 1986.

Markham, Ursula, *The Crystal Workbook*, Aquarian, 1988.

Ozaniec, Naomi, *The Elements of the Chakras*, Element Books, 1990.

Philbrock, Helen and Gregg, Richard B, *Companion Plants*, Stuart and Watkins, 1967.

Reed Gach, Michael, with Marco Carolyn, *Acu-Yoga*, Japan Publications Inc., 1981.

Sills, Franklyn, *The Polarity Process*, Element Books, 1989.

Tansley, David, *Radionics – Interface with the Ether Field*, Health Science Press, 1975.

Whitlock, Ralph, *Water Divining*, Robert Hale, 1992.

Williamson, Tom, *Dowsing: New Light on an Ancient Art*, Robert Hale, 1993.